Edmund Hodgson Yates, Frank Edward Smedley

Gathered Leaves

Being a Collection of the Poetical Writings of the Late Frank E. Smedley

Edmund Hodgson Yates, Frank Edward Smedley

Gathered Leaves
Being a Collection of the Poetical Writings of the Late Frank E. Smedley

ISBN/EAN: 9783337777951

Printed in Europe, USA, Canada, Australia, Japan

Cover: Foto ©Thomas Meinert / pixelio.de

More available books at **www.hansebooks.com**

GATHERED LEAVES:

BEING A COLLECTION OF

THE POETICAL WRITINGS

OF THE LATE

FRANK E. SMEDLEY.

WITH A

Memorial Preface

BY EDMUND YATES.

With  Illustrations.

LONDON:
VIRTUE BROTHERS & CO., 1, AMEN CORNER,
PATERNOSTER ROW.
1865.

CONTENTS.

	PAGE
"In Memoriam"	vii
Maude Allinghame; a Legend of Hertfordshire	1
Ye Right Ancient Ballad of ye Combat of King Tidrich with ye Dragon	35
The Enchanted Net	48
A Fytte of the Blues	61
The Forfeit Hand; a Legend of Brabant . .	65
The Ballad of Boreänä	90
To a Punning Beauty	94
To Mrs. G. H. Virtue	95
Valentines	96
To my Valentine	98
For M. S.	100
A Day Dream	101
Epitaph	104
Lines for Music	105

CONTENTS.

	PAGE
TO ———	106
LINES WRITTEN TO MISS AUGUSTA SHORT	109
THE LOVER'S REBUKE TO HIS HEART	111
THE HEART'S REPLY	111
THE PRAYER OF THE WEARY HEART	113
A SONG	117
LOVED BEST	119
AT HOME	121
TO L. K. Y.	122
A SERENADE	124
A REMONSTRANCE	126
"ALONE"	128
LILY FLOWER	130
SAINT PÈRE	132
A CHARACTER	134
HOPE ON, HOPE EVER!	137
ODE	139
LEBE WOHL!	144
IN VAIN	146
LINES WRITTEN FOR THE BAZAAR FOR THE WINDSOR NEW FREE AND INDUSTRIAL SCHOOLS	147

In Memoriam.

JUST about this time ten years ago, the late Mr. Bogue, the publisher, of Fleet Street, begged me to call upon him, to talk over a projected magazine which he had notions of starting. In the course of our conversation, he told me that the new periodical would have the advantage of being illustrated by glorious George Cruikshank, that it would be called "Cruikshank" Magazine," and that its literary contents would be edited by Frank Smedley, " whom of course I knew!" I was very young at that time, both in years and literature; and I recollect feeling very much humiliated as I confessed that I had never heard of the gentleman. "What?" said Mr. Bogue. "I mean

IN MEMORIAM.

the author of 'Frank Fairlegh.'" In an instant I recalled my words. Knew him? I knew him thoroughly. I had been with him in fifty rows and scrapes at his private tutor's, then followed him on in later life where we had been members of the same hunt, and taken a few bullfinches and oxers together. I had been his confidant in his love affairs, had been jealous of some of his sweethearts, and had not cared one jot for others. We had done a little racing together, and at one time had certainly "stood in" about "nobbling" an intended Derby winner. We were in Italy together, and mixed up with the *Condottieri*. I remembered an awkward affair in which we both were implicated, where a cloth was thrown over an English nobleman's head, while an Italian personage pointed to a conveniently adjacent canal. But all this friendship and *camaraderie* was on paper. I knew him only in his books! On the living man I had never set eyes in my life. So I took a letter of introduction from Mr. Bogue, and went up to Jermyn Street, where Mr. Smedley then lived, in the aspiring frame of mind befitting one about to enlist as a light free lance under a new chief. As I rode up in the cab, I was picturing to myself the man with whom I was about to become acquainted; and as I now write, those thoughts recur to me exactly as they passed through my mind. I have laughed over them so often with him who was their subject, that there is no wonder at their remaining fixed on my memory. I pictured to myself a tall, strongly-built man, of about forty years of age, bald, with a fringe of hair, large breezy whiskers, strong bony hands, and general muscular development, rather "horsy" in his dress and talk and manner. I expected that his tone would be rather *brusque*, and that I might probably be unable to attain his required standard of "knowingness" in matters relating to the field and the road. I sent in my letter, and I was ushered into the presence of a gentleman, whom, even in the dim light of a shaded lamp standing on the table by his elbow, I could tell to be suffering under some malformation, as he sat in his wheel-chair—a little man, with a peculiar, clever face; piercing eyes, never moving from the person he was addressing; a manner beginning in earnestness, and then straying into banter; a voice beginning in harshness, and modulating into pleasantest cadence; a

IN MEMORIAM.

...aring which, in its endeavour to be thoroughly independent, seemed leaning towards repulsion, and yet which—spite of itself, as it seemed—was indefinably attractive. I was so astonished at finding such a difference in what I had expected, that, as I have since thought, my answers to his short and pertinent questions must have been vague and unsatisfactory. At all events, I recollect that my new acquaintance's tone became slightly sarcastic, which recalled me to myself; that I endeavoured to answer him as best I could; that his manner then changed; and that on that, the first day of our acquaintance, we formed an intimate friendship, which continued until the latest hour of his life.

I think that this kindness of heart, veiled occasionally under an affectation of worldly-mindedness, and a little cynicism very badly sustained, was the ruling spirit of his life. He was never happy save when doing a kindness to some one—never pleased save when he had some little pet scheme of beneficence, which he would bring out as though he were ashamed of it; while his quivering lips and brimming eyes belied the assumed roughness of his voice and manner.

IN MEMORIAM.

He was soft-hearted to a degree; indeed, converse with him had a sanctifying and hallowing influence. His physical malady had kept his intercourse with the world so restricted, that while his mind was full, strong, and manly, his experiences of certain sides of life were as pure and unsullied as those of a young girl. All the impulses of his soul were deep-set, earnest, fervent, and generous. He had heard of the lower views of humanity held by some great men, but he had never had reason to allow their existence; so he frankly and unhesitatingly denied it. He was himself a man "in whom was no guile," and it was very difficult indeed for him to allow its presence in any one else. With all the masculinity of his writings (and it is allowed that there are very few writers who, in certain phases of description, notably of the hunting-field and the race-course, have ever equalled, while certainly none have ever surpassed him), his mind was, to a certain degree, feminine. He had the strong likings and dislikings, petulances, love of small jokes, desire of praise, and irritation at small annoyances, which are frequently found in women; but, on the other hand, he had a magnanimity, an amount of patient

IN MEMORIAM.

long-suffering, and a courage both moral and physical, such as are given to few men. I, the writer of this imperfect sketch, knew, I believe, most of the secret aspirations of his heart; and I look back upon him as, mentally, a perfect type of the romantic knights of old—capable of a devoted, unselfish love; worshipping woman as a being worthy of all honour, and almost incapable of wrong; delighting in feats of horsemanship and daring; of unsullied honour and unswerving integrity, impatient of double-dealing; impetuous, yet easily guided; simple-minded, and of fervent faith. His bodily infirmities, before alluded to, prevented him from indulging in any of the amusements which he most fancied, shut him out from a vast amount of society, kept him a prisoner to his chair; and yet I never heard one syllable of repining escape his lips, though on more than one occasion I have heard him turn off some well-meant though badly-timed commiseration with a light-hearted jest.

Of some authors it may be said that their lives are written in their books, but Frank Smedley's works reveal no glimpse of his actual life. Here and there one finds in them sketches of his personal friends,

IN MEMORIAM.

pleasant reproductions, so kindly brought out that the originals always enjoyed them most. Here and there one comes across bits of observation and reflection, such as his intimates have heard him utter; but for the most part his novels are but the vent for that extraordinary fund of high animal spirits which, under other circumstances, would have been brought into play in adventure, in sporting, in fighting the great battle of life. But in some of the minor poems scattered throughout this volume the reader will find many little passages in which my poor friend evidently refers to his own afflicted condition, but never without patient resignation and fervent hope—two virtues illustrated in every action of his daily life.

Springing from a good old English family, who, for the last two or three generations, have had intimate relations with Westminster School (his grandfather and his cousin were well-known masters there, and there his father had been educated), FRANCIS EDWARD SMEDLEY was born on the 4th October, 1818, at Marlow. At his birth he was a remarkably fine child; but it pleased God to afflict him with some strange malady, which could never find a technical name, nor

IN MEMORIAM.

be thoroughly accounted for by the members of the faculty, but which retarded his growth, and delayed his physical development. Under these circumstances it was considered advisable that his earliest studies should be pursued at home; and it was not until he was fourteen years of age that he was placed under the care of a private tutor, the Rev. Charles Millett, resident at Brighton. In Mr. Millett's house he remained for some months; but his health was found incompatible with even the comparatively mild boy-roughness to be found at a private tutor's; and he returned home to pursue his studies under the eye of his cousin, the Rev. E. A. Smedley, one of the Westminster masters before mentioned. When his education was completed, he more keenly than ever felt the pressure of those sad circumstances which prevented him from following one of the several callings for young men of position and education, but he accepted his lot with that cheerful resignation which never forsook him. And then, at that which was perhaps the darkest period of his life, came the dawning of what may be considered its brightest and happiest phase, his literary career. Two ladies, his cousins, one of whom has since attained a distinguished name as an authoress, had noticed that Frank Smedley had a very acute perception of the ludicrous, and that his correspondence with them was marked by power of character-reading and graphic description such as is rarely met with. As a means of employment, and of allaying that listless depression under which he at times necessarily suffered, they suggested that he should attempt to delineate some of his own experiences of life. These had been small enough; but from them he managed to extract an entire novelty. As he himself says in his preface to "Frank Fairlegh," "while volume after volume had been devoted to 'schoolboy days,' and 'college life,' the mysteries of that paradise of public-school-fearing mammas, a 'private tutor's,' yet continued unrevealed." To him fell the task of their revelation. His experiences at Mr. Millett's gave him the substratum of fact; his brilliant fancy supplied the rest; and the "Scenes from the Life of a Private Pupil," contributed to "Sharpe's London Magazine" (then a popular periodical), were so successful, that the proprietor of the miscellany suggested an extension of the series

IN MEMORIAM.

originally contemplated, and finally published them in a complete form, under the title of "Frank Fairlegh."

In the dedication of the book he thus thanks the ladies, his cousins, who first prompted his labour:— "As it is mainly owing to your joint advice and encouragement that this tale has been either written or laid before the public, there can be none to whom I may with greater propriety dedicate it. When I add that my satisfaction in making the slight acknowledgment of the countless acts of affectionate kindness I have received at your hands, is one among the many agreeable results of the advice which has eventually led me to adopt a literary career, you will not refuse to accept this assurance that you have contributed to the happiness of one whose sphere, both of duties and of pleasures, Providence has seen fit to limit."

In the pages of the same magazine he published his second, the longest and perhaps most popular of his works, entitled, "Lewis Arundel; or, the Railroad of Life," which, although the story is somewhat drawn out and several unnecessary characters are introduced,

IN MEMORIAM.

contains some bits of descriptive writing which are truly admirable. While this story was in progress he assumed the editorial guidance of "Sharpe's Magazine," at the request of Mr. Sharpe, the then proprietor, discharging his duties gratuitously at first, until the magazine became the property of Mr. Virtue; and to it, besides the leading serial tale, he contributed many short sketches, and some very quaintly humorous comments on, and replies to, the correspondence he received in his judicial capacity. A Christmas story, called "The Fortunes of the Colville Family," was also published by Mr. Smedley about this time.

"Cruikshank's Magazine," alluded to in the opening of this sketch, was a failure. I can scarcely tell why. In his best days the veteran draughtsman had never designed a more telling picture than the "Tail of a Comet," which formed the frontispiece of the first number, nor carried one out with more elaboration of detail. But Frank Smedley did not contribute any story; merely confined himself to what is technically known as "writing up to cuts," and the rest of us were young beginners without any literary reputation. So, after the third number, "Cruikshank's Magazine" was

IN MEMORIAM.

given up, and shortly afterwards Frank Smedley undertook another flight, a flight at that time only undertaken by Messrs. Dickens, Thackeray, Lever, and himself—the issue of a novel in monthly parts.

His story, which commenced most auspiciously, was called "Harry Coverdale's Courtship," and was illustrated in the approved form with two steel engravings by Phiz. It was hailed with warm commendation by the press, and promised to be its author's most complete and compact work—more, indeed, of a thorough character-novel than any he had yet attempted. But illness prevented the carrying out of the scheme with that vigour which had characterised its commencement. He completed his book, but not in the manner he had wished. In the preface he himself says, "The conclusion of the tale has been perpetrated at a time when, on account of severe nervous headaches, the author was under strict medical orders not to write a line upon any consideration; and it is with the fear of the doctor before his eyes that he is penning these few last words. They are not written in the forlorn hope of disarming criticism, but simply to assure those friends who have hitherto looked with an indulgent eye on his

IN MEMORIAM.

writings, that if 'Harry Coverdale's Courtship' does not come up to the expectations they may have formed from the perusals of his previous works, it is rather the misfortune than the fault of their grateful and obedient servant, the author." While his novel was in progress he had published in conjunction with me a little shilling book of nonsense verses, called "Mirth and Metre," his share of which is here reprinted, and this, with the exception of a few papers contributed out of friendship to me to the "Train," a magazine of which I was editor, was the last of his published works. His health, always delicate, declined very much; he became a victim to intense headaches, violent and of long duration, which were caused, doubtless, by an accident which happened to him in the autumn of '56, when he was thrown from his pony-carriage, and dragged for some distance along the road before the pony could be stopped; and as, by a change in his circumstances, anything like necessity for writing had been done away with, he gave himself up, when he was free from suffering, to tranquil leisure and lettered ease. He read much, and of all kinds, and he was never happier than when, surrounded by a few old friends, he led the discussion upon books

IN MEMORIAM.

and their authors. After his father's death, which happened some six years ago, he continued living with his mother at Grove Lodge, Regent's Park—a house the grounds of which are perhaps the most perfect realisation of the *rus in urbe* ever met with, where, if he chose, he could get fresh air without being wheeled out of the tranquil precincts of his garden, and where he was in the immediate neighbourhood of the Zoological Gardens, his favourite resort. But about two years since he purchased for himself a charming estate called Beechwood, within a very short distance of Marlow, his native place; and here he had passed the two last summers of his life, thoroughly happy, and, as we all fondly hoped, gaining strength and health.

On Thursday, the 28th of April, in this current year, I dined with him at Grove Lodge, and thought him better and brighter than I had seen him for some length of time. When the other guests left the dinner-table he asked me to remain, and talked to me with the greatest spirit and interest about the work on which I was then engaged, about some horses he had bought, about his desire to get away speedily into the country and enjoy all the beauties of the coming summer—about

IN MEMORIAM.

a dozen little trifles, into all of which he entered with even more than his ordinary zest. I left him, promising to return the next week and settle an early date for visiting him at Beechwood. On Sunday morning, the 1st of May, he was found by his servant, who came to call him, in a state of stupor, speedily followed by a succession of epileptic fits, and by Sunday evening he was dead. On Monday, the 9th of May, we laid his mortal remains in Marlow churchyard, between the church where

> "The kneeling hamlet drains
> The chalice of the grapes of God,"

and the river which he loved so well. The shops in the little-town were all closed, and though the weather was most tempestuous, the churchyard was filled with the townspeople, who had all known and esteemed the kind-hearted, cheerful spirit who had lately sojourned amongst them, whose dire malady had never soured his temper, but who always had a pleasant word and a merry jest for those who passed him as he travelled to and from the town in his wheel-chair. All peace to his ashes! The calm tranquillity of Marlow churchyard

IN MEMORIAM.

will not be less endeared to the lover of the picturesque because it contains the mortal remains of one who ministered in his life to the innocent amusement of his fellow-creatures, and who with the spirit of a man combined the simplicity of a child.

EDMUND YATES.

Kensington, *December*, 1864.

MAUDE ALLINGHAME;

A LEGEND OF HERTFORDSHIRE.*

Part the First.

HERE is weeping and wailing in Allinghame Hall,
From many an eye does the tear-drop fall,

---

* The following legend is founded on a story current in the part of Herts where the scene is laid; the house was actually burnt down about ten years ago, having just been rendered habitable:

GATHERED LEAVES.

Swollen with sorrow is many a lip,
Many a nose is red at the tip;
All the shutters are shut very tight,
To keep out the wind and to keep out the light;

While a couple of mutes,
With very black suits,
And extremely long faces,
Have taken their places

GATHERED LEAVES.

With an air of professional *esprit de corps*,
One on each side of the great hall door.
On the gravel beyond, in a wonderful state
Of black velvet and feathers, a grand hearse, and eight
Magnificent horses, the orders await
      Of a spruce undertaker,
        Who's come from Long Acre,
To furnish a coffin, and do the polite
To the corpse of Sir Reginald Allinghame, Knight.

The lamented deceased whose funeral arrangement
I've just been describing, resembled that strange gent
Who ventured to falsely imprison a great man,
Viz. the Ottoman captor of noble Lord Bateman;
For we're told in that ballad which makes our eyes
    water,
That this terrible Turk had got one only daughter;
And although our good knight had twice seen twins
    arrive, a
Young lady named Maude was the only survivor.
      So there being no entail
        On some horrid heir-male,
And no far-away cousin or distant relation
To lay claim to the lands and commence litigation,
'Tis well known through the county, by each one and all
That fair Maude is the heiress of Allinghame Hall.

GATHERED LEAVES.

Yes! she was very fair to view;
Mark well that forehead's ivory hue,
That speaking eye, whose glance of pride
The silken lashes scarce can hide,
E'en when, as now, its wonted fire
Is paled with weeping o'er her sire;
Those scornful lips, that part to show
The pearl-like teeth in even row;
That dimpled chin, so round and fair,
The clusters of her raven hair,
Whose glossy curls their shadow throw
O'er her smooth brow and neck of snow;
The faultless hand, the ankle small,
The figure more than woman tall,
And yet so graceful, sculptor's art
Such symmetry could ne'er impart.
Observe her well, and then confess
The power of female loveliness,
And say, " Except a touch of vice
   One may descry
   About the eye,
 Rousing a Caudle-ish recollection,
 Which might perchance upon reflection
 Turn out a serious objection,
That gal would make '*a heavenly splice.*'"

GATHERED LEAVES.

  From far and wide
  On every side
 The county did many a suitor ride,
Who, wishing to marry, determined to call
And propose for the heiress of Allinghame Hall.
 Knights who'd gather'd great fame in
 Stabbing, cutting, and maiming
 The French and their families
 At Blenheim and Ramilies,
 In promiscuous manslaughter
 T'other side of the water,
 Very eagerly sought her;
 Yet, though presents they brought her,
 And fain would have taught her,
To fancy they loved her, not one of them caught her.
Maude received them all civilly, asked them to dine,
Gave them capital venison, and excellent wine,
But declared, when they popp'd, that she'd really no notion
They'd had serious intentions—she own'd their devotion
Was excessively flattering—quite touching—in fact
She was grieved at the part duty forced her to act;
Still her recent bereavement—her excellent father—
(Here she took out her handkerchief)—yes, she had rather—

GATHERED LEAVES.

Rather not (here she sobb'd) say a thing so unpleasant,
But she'd made up her mind not to marry at present.
Might she venture to hope that she still should retain
Their friendship?—to lose that would cause her *such*
     pain.
Would they like to take supper?—she fear'd etiquette,
         A thing not to be set
At defiance by one in her sad situation,
Having no "Maiden Aunt," or old moral relation
         Of orthodox station,
         Whose high reputation,
         And prim notoriety,
         Should inspire society
With a very deep sense of the strictest propriety;
Such a relative wanting, she feared, so she said,
Etiquette must prevent her from offering a bed;
But the night was so fine, just the thing for a ride—
Must they go? Well, good-bye,—and here once more
     she sigh'd;
Then a last parting smile on the suitor she threw,
And thus, having "let him down easy," withdrew,
While the lover rode home with an indistinct notion
That somehow he'd not taken much by his motion.

         Young Lord Dandelion,
         An illustrious scion,

A green sprig of nobility,
Whose excessive gentility
I fain would describe if I had but ability,—
This amiable lordling, being much in the state
I've described, *i.e.* going home at night rather late,
Having got his *congé*
(As a Frenchman would say)
From the heiress, with whom he'd been anxious to
  mate,
Is jogging along, in a low state of mind,
When a horseman comes rapidly up from behind,
And a voice in his ear
Shouts in tones round and clear,
"Ho, there! stand and deliver! your money or life!"
While some murderous weapon, a pistol or knife,
Held close to his head,
As these words are being said,
Glitters cold in the moonlight, and fills him with dread.

Now I think you will own,
That when riding alone
On the back of a horse, be it black, white, or roan,
Or chestnut, or bay,
Or piebald, or grey,
Or dun-brown (though a notion my memory crosses
That 'tis asses are usually done brown, not horses),

GATHERED LEAVES.

When on horseback, I say, in the dead of the night,
        Nearly dark, if not quite,
        In despite of the light
        Of the moon shining bright-
ish—yes, not more than -ish, for the planet's cold rays I
've been told on this night were unusually hazy—
        With no one in sight,
        To the left or the right,
Save a well-mounted highwayman fully intent
On obtaining your money, as Dan did his rent,
By bullying—an odd sort of annual pleasantry
That "Repaler" play'd off on the finest of peasantry;
In so awkward a fix I should certainly say,
        By far the best way
Is to take matters easy, and quietly pay;
The alternative being that the robber may treat us
To a couple of bullets by way of *quietus;*
Thus applying our brains, if perchance we have got any,
In this summary mode to the study of botany,
By besprinkling the leaves, and the grass, and the
    flowers,
With the source of our best intellectual powers,
And, regardless of *habeas corpus,* creating
A feast for the worms, which are greedily waiting
        Till such time as any gent
        Quits this frail tenement,

And adopting a shroud as his sole outer garment,
Becomes food for worms, slugs, and all such-like varmint.

  My Lord Dandelion,
  That illustrious scion,
Not possessing the pluck of the bold hero Brian
(Of whom Irishmen rave till one murmurs "How true
Is the brute's patronymic of Brian *Bore you*"),
  Neither feeling inclined,
  Nor having a mind
To be shot by a highwayman, merely said, "Eh?
Aw—extwemely unpleasant—aw—take it, sir, pway;"
And without further parley his money resign'd.

  Away! away!
  With a joyous neigh,
Bounds the highwayman's steed, like a colt at play;
And a merry laugh rings loud and clear,
On the terrified drum of his trembling ear,
While the following words doth his lordship hear:—
  "Unlucky, my lord; unlucky, I know,
   For the money to go
   And the heiress say 'No,'
On the self-same day, is a terrible blow.

GATHERED LEAVES.

When next you visit her, good my lord,
Give THE HIGHWAYMAN'S love to fair Mistress Maude!"

    Away! away!
  On his gallant grey
    My Lord Dandelion,
    That unfortunate scion,
Gallops as best he may;
And as he rides he mutters low,
"Insolent fellar, how did *he* know?"

In the stable department of Allinghame Hall
    There's the devil to pay,
    As a body may say,
And no assets forthcoming to answer the call;
    For the head groom, Roger,
    A knowing old codger,
    In a thundering rage,
    Which nought can assuage,
    Most excessively cross is
    With the whole stud of horses,
    While he viciously swears
    At the fillies and mares;
He bullies the helpers, he kicks all the boys,
Upsets innocent pails with superfluous noise;
Very loudly doth fret and incessantly fume,

GATHERED LEAVES.

And behaves, in a word,
In a way most absurd,
More befitting a madman, by far, than a groom,
Till at length he finds vent
For his deep discontent
In the following soliloquy :—" I'm blest if this is
To be stood any longer; I'll go and tell Missis;
If she don't know some dodge as 'll stop this here rig,
Vy then, dash my vig,
This here werry morning
I jest gives her warning,
If I don't I'm a Dutchman, or summut as worse is."
Then, after a short obligato of curses,
Just to let off the steam, Roger dons his best clothes,
And seeks his young mistress his griefs to disclose.

" Please your Ladyship's Honour
I've come here upon a
Purtiklar rum business going on in the stable,
Vich, avake as I am, I ain't no how been able
To get at the truth on :—the last thing each night
I goes round all the 'orses to see as they're right,—
And they alvays *is* right too, as far as I see,
Cool, kviet, and clean, just as 'orses should be,—
Then, furst thing ev'ry morning agen I goes round,
To see as the cattle is all safe and sound.

GATHERED LEAVES.

'Twas nigh three veeks ago, or perhaps rather more,
Ven vun morning, as usual, I unlocks the door—
 Tho' I ought to ha' mention'd I alvays does lock it,
And buttons the key in my right breeches pocket —
I opens the door, Marm, and there vas Brown Bess,
Your ladyship's mare, in a horribul mess;
Reg'lar kiver'd all over vith sveat, foam, and lather,
Laying down in her stall—sich a sight for a father!
Vhile a saddle and bridle, as hung there kvite clean
Over night, vas all mud and not fit to be seen;
And, to dock a long tale, since that day thrice a-
  week,
Or four times, perhaps, more or less, so to speak,
  I've diskivered that thare
  Identical mare,
Or else the black barb,—vich, perhaps you'll remember
Vas brought here from over the seas last September,—
In the state I describes, as if fairies or vitches
Had rode 'em all night over hedges and ditches;
If this here's to go on (and I'm sure I don't know
How to stop it), I tells you at vunce, I must go;
  Yes, although I've lived here
  A good twenty-five year,
I am sorry to say (for I knows what your loss is),
You must get some vun else to look arter your
  'orses."

GATHERED LEAVES.

      Roger's wonderful tale
      Seem'd of little avail,
For Maude neither fainted, nor scream'd, nor turn'd pale,
But she sign'd with her finger to bid him draw near;
      And cried, " Roger, come here,
      I've a word for your ear;"
      Then she whisper'd so low
      That I really don't know
What it was that she said, but it seem'd *apropos*
      And germane to the matter;
      For though Roger stared at her,
      With mouth wide asunder,
      Extended by wonder,
Ere she ended, his rage appear'd wholly brought under,
      Insomuch that the groom,
      When he quitted the room,
Louted low, and exclaim'd, with a grin of delight,
" Your Ladyship's Honour's a gentleman quite!"
'Tis reported, that night, at the sign of "The Goat,"
Roger the groom changed a £20 note.

GATHERED LEAVES.

Part the Second.

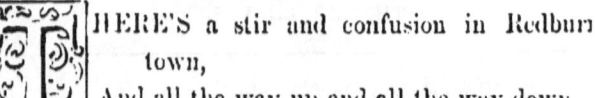

THERE'S a stir and confusion in Redburn
    town,
And all the way up and all the way down

    The principal street,
    When the neighbours meet,
They do nothing but chafe, and grumble, and frown,
    And sputter and mutter,
    And sentences utter,

GATHERED LEAVES.

Such as these—" Have you heard,
　　The thing that's occurr'd?
　　His worship the Mayor?
　　Shocking affair!
　　Much too bad, I declare!
　　Fifty pounds, I've been told!
　　And as much more in gold.
　　Well, the villain *is* bold!
　　Two horse pistols!—No more?
　　I thought they said four.
　　And so close to the town!
　　I say, Gaffer Brown,
　　Do tell us about it."
　　" Thus the matter fell out—it
Was only last night that his worship the Mayor,
　　Master Zachary Blair,
Having been at St. Alban's and sold in the fair
Some fifteen head of cattle, a horse and a mare,
　　Jogging home on his nag
　　With the cash in a bag,
Was met by a highwayman arm'd to the teeth,
With a belt full of pistols and sword in its
　　sheath,
　　A murderous villain, six feet high,
　　With spur on heel and boot on thigh,
　　And a great black beard and a wicked eye;

And he said to his Worship, 'My fat little friend,
    I will thank you to lend
Me that nice bag of gold, which no doubt you intend
    Before long to expend
    In some awfully slow way,
    Or possibly low way,
Which I should not approve. Come, old fellow, be
    quick!'
And then Master Blair heard an ominous click,
    Betokening the cocking
    Of a pistol, a shocking
    Sound, which caused him to quake,
    And shiver and shake,
From the crown of his head to the sole of his stocking.
    So yielding himself with a touching submission
    To what he consider'd a vile imposition,
He handed the bag with the tin to the highway-
man, who took it, and saying, in rather a dry way,
'Many thanks, gallant sir,' gallop'd off down a by-way."

The town council has met, and his worship the Mayor,
    Master Zachary Blair,
    Having taken the chair,
And sat in it too, which was nothing but fair,
    Did at once, then and there,
    Relate and declare,

GATHERED LEAVES.

With a dignified air,
And a presence most rare,
The tale we've just heard, which made all men to stare,
And indignantly swear,
It was too bad to bear.
Then after they'd fully discuss'd the affair,
To find out the best method of setting things square,
They agreed one and all the next night to repair,
Upon horseback, or mare,
To the highwayman's lair,
And, if he appear'd, hunt him down like a hare.

Over No-Man's-Land* the moon shines bright,
And the furze and the fern in its liquid light
Glitter and gleam of a silvery white;
The lengthen'd track which the cart-wheels make,
Winds o'er the heath like a mighty snake,
And silence o'er that lonely wold
Doth undisputed empire hold,
Save where the night-breeze fitfully
Mourns like some troubled spirit's cry;
At the cross roads the old sign-post
Shows dimly forth, like sheeted ghost,

---

* The name of a lonely common near Harpenden, formerly a favourite site for prize-fights.

As with weird arm, extended still,
It points the road to Leamsford Mill;
 In fact it is not
 At all a sweet spot,
 A nice situation,
 Or charming location;
The late Robins himself, in despite his vocation,
 Would have deem'd this a station
 Unworthy laudation,
And have probably term'd it "a blot on the nation."

 In a lane hard by,
 Where the hedge-rows high,
Veil with their leafy boughs the sky,
Biding their time, sits his worship the Mayor,
 Master Zachary Blair,
 And my Lord Dandelion,
 That illustrious scion,
And Oxley the butcher, and Doughy the baker,
And Chisel the joiner and cabinet-maker,
 And good farmer Dacre,
 Who holds many an acre,
And, *insuper omnes*, bold Jonathan Blaker,
 The famous thief-taker,
Who's been sent for from town as being more wide-
  awak*er*,

GATHERED LEAVES.

(Excuse that comparative, sure 'tis no crime
To sacrifice grammar to such a nice rhyme),
And up to the dodges of fellows who take a
Delight in being born in "stone jugs," and then take a-
way all their lives long in a manner would make a
Live Archbishop to swear, let alone any Quaker,
Wet or dry, you can name, or a Jumper or Shaker;
And, to add to this list, Hobbs was there, so was Dobbs,
With several others, all more or less snobs,
Low partys, quite willing to peril their nobs
In highwayman catching, and such-like odd jobs,
To obtain a few shillings, which they would term bobs.

   'Tisn't pleasant to wait
   In a fidgety state
 Of mind, at an hour we deem very late,
  When our fancies have fled
  Home to supper and bed,
And we feel we are catching a cold in the head;
(By the way, if this ailment should ever make you ill,
Drop some neat sal-volatile into your gruel,
   You'll be all right next day,
   And will probably say,
This, by way of receipt, is a regular jewel);
   To wait, I repeat,
   For a robber or cheat,

On a spot he's supposed to select for his beat,
When said robber wont come 's the reverse of a treat.

So thought the butcher, and so thought the baker,
And so thought the joiner and cabinet-maker,
And so thought all the rest except Jonathan Blaker;
To him catching a thief in the dead of the night
Presented a source of unfailing delight;
  And now as he sat
  Peering under his hat,
He looked much like a terrier watching a rat.

  Hark! he hears a muffled sound;
 He slips from the saddle, his ear's to the ground.
  Louder and clearer,
  Nearer and nearer,
'Tis a horse's tramp on the soft green sward!
He is mounted again: "Now, good my Lord,
Now, master Mayor, mark well, if you can,
A rider approaches, is this your man?"

Ay, mark that coal-black barb that skims,
With flowing mane and graceful limbs,
As lightly onward o'er the lea
As greyhound from the leash set free;

GATHERED LEAVES.

Observe the rider's flashing eye,
His gallant front and bearing high;
His slender form, which scarce appears
Fitted to manhood's riper years;
The easy grace with which at need
He checks or urges on his steed;
Can this be one whose fame is spread
For deeds of rapine and of dread?

My Lord Dandelion
Placed his spy-glass his eye on,
Stared hard at the rider, and then exclaim'd, "Well—
ar—
'Tis weally *so* dark! but I think 'tis the fellar."
While his worship the Mayor
Whisper'd, "Oh, look ye there!
That purse in his girdle, d'ye see it?—I twigg'd it;
'Tis my purse as was prigg'd, and the willin what prigg'd it!"

Hurrah! hurrah!
He's off and away,
Follow who can, follow who may.
There's hunting and chasing
And going the pace in
Despite of the light, which is not good for racing.

GATHERED LEAVES.

"Hold hard! hold hard! there's somebody spilt,
      And entirely kilt!"
      "Well, never mind,
      Leave him behind,"—
The pace is a great deal too good to be kind.
      Follow, follow,
      O'er hill and hollow,—
      Faster, faster,
      Another disaster!
His worship the Mayor has got stuck in a bog.
And there let us leave him to spur and to flog,
He'll know better the next time,—a stupid old dog!
      "Where's Hobbs?"
      "I don't know."
      "And Dobbs and the snobs?"
      "All used-up long ago."
      "My nag's almost blown!"
      "And mine's got a stone
In his shoe—I'm afraid it's no go. Why, I say!
That rascally highwayman's getting away!"

'Tis true. Swift as the trackless wind,
The gallant barb leaves all behind;
Hackney and hunter still in vain
Exert each nerve, each sinew strain;

GATHERED LEAVES.

And all in vain that motley crew
Of horsemen still the chase pursue.
Two by two, and one by one,
They lag behind—'tis nearly done,
That desperate game, that eager strife,
That fearful race for death or life.
Those dark trees gain'd that skirt the moor,
All danger of pursuit is o'er;
Screen'd by their shade from every eye,
Escape becomes a certainty.
Haste! for with stern, relentless will
ONE RIDER'S ON THY TRACES STILL!

'Tis bold Jonathan Bla-
ker who sticks to his prey
In this somewhat unfeeling, though business-like way.
But even he, too, is beginning to find
That the pace is so good he'll be soon left behind.
He presses his horse on with hand and with heel,
He rams in the persuaders too hard a great deal;
'Tis but labour in vain,
Though he starts from the pain,
Nought can give that stout roadster his wind back again.

GATHERED LEAVES.

Now Jonathan Blaker had formerly been
A soldier, and fought for his country and queen,
Over seas, the Low Countries to wit, and while
    there, in
      Despite of good teaching,
      And praying and preaching,
Had acquired a shocking bad habit of swear-
    ing;
      Thus, whenever, as now,
      The red spot on his brow
      Proved him "wrathy and riled,"
      He would not draw it mild,
But would, sans apology, let out on such
    Occasions a torrent of very low Dutch.
One can scarce feel surprise, then, considering the
    urgency
Of the case, that he cried in the present emergency,
"*Ach donner und blitzen*" (a taste of his lingo),
"He'll escape, by ——" (I don't know the German for
    "jingo")
      "*Tausend teufel! sturmwetter!*
      To think I should let a
Scamp like that get away; don't I wish now that I'd
    ha'
Drove a brace of lead pills through the horse or the
    rider;

P'r'aps there's time for it still—*Mein auge* (my eye),
'Tis the only chance left, so here goes for a try."

    Oh, faster spur thy flagging steed,
    Still faster,—fearful is thy need.
    Oh, heed not now his failing breath,
    Life lies before, behind thee death!
    Warning all vainly given! too late
    To shield thee from the stroke of fate.
    One glance the fierce pursuer threw,
    A pistol from his holster drew,
    Levell'd and fired, the echoes still
    Prolong the sound from wood to hill;
    But ere the last vibrations die,
    A WOMAN'S shriek of agony
    Rings out beneath that midnight sky!

The household sleep soundly in Allinghame Hall,
Groom, butler, and coachman, cook, footboy, and all;
    The fat old housekeeper
    (Never was such a sleeper),
    After giving a snore,
    Which was almost a roar,
Has just turn'd in her bed and begun a fresh score;

The butler (a shocking old wine-bibbing sinner),
Having made some mistake after yesterday's dinner,
As to where he should put a decanter of sherry,

    Went to bed rather merry,
    But perplexed in his mind,
    Not being able to find
    A legitimate reason
    Why at that time and season
His *eight*-post bed chooses, whichever way he stirs,
To present to his vision a *couple* of testers!

GATHERED LEAVES.

Since which, still more completely his spirits to damp,
He'd been roused twice by nightmare and three times
    by cramp!
    And now he dreams some old church-bell
    Is mournfully tolling a dead man's knell,
And he starts in his sleep, and mutters, "Alas!
    Man's life's brittle as glass!
There's another cork flown, and the spirit escaped;
    Heigh ho!" (here he gaped),
    Then, scratching his head,
    He sat up in bed,
For that bell goes on ringing more loud than before,
And he knows 'tis the bell of the great hall door.
    Footman tall,
    Footboy small,
    Housekeeper, butler, coachman, and all,
In a singular state of extreme dishabille,
    Which they each of them feel
    Disinclined to reveal,
And yet know not very well how to conceal,
    With one accord rush to the old oak hall;
    To unfasten the door
    Takes a minute or more
It opens at length and discloses a sight
Which fills them with wonder, and sorrow, and
    fright.

GATHERED LEAVES.

The ruddy light of early dawn
Gilds with its rays that velvet lawn;
From every shrub and painted flower
Dew-drops distil in silvery shower;
Sweet perfumes load the air; the song
Of waking birds is borne along
Upon the bosom of the breeze
That murmurs through the waving trees;
The crystal brook that dances by
Gleams in the sunlight merrily;
All tells of joy, and love, and life—
All?—Said I everything was rife
With happiness?—Behold that form,
Like lily broken by the storm,
Fall'n prostrate on the steps before
The marble threshold of the door!
The well-turned limbs, the noble mien,
The riding-coat of Lincoln green;
The hat, whose plume of sable hue,
Its shadow o'er his features threw;
Yon coal-black barb, too, panting near,
All show some youthful cavalier;
While, fatal evidence of strife,
From a deep hurt the flood of life
Proves, as its current stains the sod,
How man defiles the work of God.

GATHERED LEAVES.

With eager haste the servants raise
The head, and on the features gaze,
Then backward start in sad surprise
As that pale face they recognise.
Good reason theirs, although, in sooth,
They knew but half the fatal truth;
For, strange as doth the tale appear,
One startling fact is all too clear,
The robber, who on No-Man's-Land
Was shot by Blaker's ruthless hand,—
That highwayman of evil fame
Is beauteous Maude of Allinghame!

L'ENVOI.

"Well, but that's not the end?"
"Yes it is, my good friend."
"Oh, I say!
That won't pay;
'Tis a shocking bad way
To leave off so abruptly. I wanted to hear
A great many particulars: first, I'm not clear,
Is the young woman killed?" "Be at rest on that head,
She's completely defunct, most excessively dead.

GATHERED LEAVES.

Blaker's shot did the business; she'd just strength to fly,
Reach'd her home, rang the bell, and then sank down
　　to die."
" Poor girl! really it's horrid! However, I knew it
Could come to no good—I felt certain she'd rue it—
But pray, why in the world did the jade go to do it?"
" 'Tis not easy to say; but at first, I suppose,
Just by way of a freak she rode out in man's clothes."
" Then her taking the money?" "A mere idiosyn-
　　crasy,
As when, some years since, a young gent, being with
　　drink crazy,
Set off straight on end to the British Museum,
And, having arrived there, transgress'd all the laws
Of good breeding, by smashing the famed Portland
　　Vase!
Or the shop-lifting ladies, by dozens you see 'em,
For despising the diff'rence 'twixt tuum and meum,
Brought before the Lord Mayor every week, in the
　　papers.
　　　　　Why, the chief linen-drapers
Have a man in their shops solely paid for revealing
When they can't keep their fair hands from picking and
　　stealing.
'Twas a mere woman's fancy, a female caprice,
And you know at that time they'd no rural police."

GATHERED LEAVES.

"Hum! it *may* have been so. Well, is that all about it?"
"No; there's more to be told, though I daresay you'll doubt it-
s being true; but the story goes on to relate,
That after Maude's death, the old Hall and estate
Were put up to auction, and Master Blair thought it
Seem'd a famous investment, bid for it and bought it,
And fitted it up in extremely bad taste;
      But scarce had he placed
His foot o'er the threshold,—the very first night,
      He woke up in a fright,
Being roused from his sleep by a terrible cry
Of 'Fire!'—had only a minute to fly
In his shirt, Mrs. Blair in her——Well, never mind,
In the dress she had on at the time: while behind
Follow'd ten little blessings, who looked very winning,
In ten little nightgowns of Irish linen;
They'd just time to escape, when the flames with a roar
Like thunder, burst forth from each window and door;
      And there, with affright,
      They perceive by the light
      Maude Allinghame's sprite—
Her real positive ghost—no fantastic illusion
Conceived by their brains from the smoke and confusion—

GATHERED LEAVES.

With a hot flaming brand
In each shadowy hand,
Flaring up, like a fiend, in the midst of the fire,
And exciting the flames to burn fiercer and higher.
From what follows we learn that ghosts, spirits, and
　　elves,
Are the creatures of habit as well as ourselves;
For Maude (that is, ghost Maude), when once she had
　　done
The trick, seem'd to think it was capital fun;
And whenever the house is rebuilt, and prepared
For a tenant, the rooms being all well scrubb'd and
　　air'd,
The very first night the new owner arrives
Maude's implacable spirit still ever contrives
　　　Many various ways in
　　　To set it a blazing;
　　　In this way she's done
　　　Both the Phœnix and Sun
So especially brown by the fires she's lighted,
　　　That now, being invited
To grant an insurance, they always say when a nice
　　　Offer is made them,
　　　'Tis no use to persuade them,
If a ghost's in the case, they won't do it at any
　　price."

GATHERED LEAVES.

MORAL.

And now for the moral! *Imprimis*, young heiresses,
Don't go riding o' nights, and don't rob mayors or
  mayoresses;
As to robbing your suitors, allow me to say,
On the face of the thing 'tis a scheme that won't pay;
Though they sigh and protest, and are dabs at love-
  making,
      You'll not find one in ten
      Of these charming young men
Can produce on occasion a purse worth your taking.
Don't refuse a good offer, but think ere you let a
Chance like that slip away, *that you mayn't get a better*.
      One more hint and I've done—
      If by pistol or gun
      It should e'er be your lot
      (Which I hope it may not),
      In a row to get shot,
And the doctor's assistance should all prove in vain,
"When you give up the ghost, don't resume it again."
If you *do* choose to "walk" and revisit this earth
To play tricks, let some method be mixed with your
  mirth.
As to burning down houses and ruining folks,

GATHERED LEAVES.

And flaring about like a Fire-king's daughter,—
Allow me to say there's no fun in such jokes,
    'Twould far better have been
    To have copied Undine,—
There's no harm in a mixture of *spirits and water!*

GATHERED LEAVES.

Yᴱ RIGHT ANCIENT BALLAD
OF
Yᴱ COMBAT OF KING TIDRICA WITH Yᴱ DRAGON.

Ye Peroration.

EY for the march of intellect,
　The schoolmaster's abroad,
　And still the cry is raised on high,

GATHERED LEAVES.

Obey his mighty word!
Where'er we go, both high and low,
  Bow down before his nod;
And the sceptre may hide its jewell'd pride,
  For our sceptre's the birchen rod.

And all "enlighten'd citizens" and "learned brothers"
  say,
    That the world was never
    One half so clever
As it is in the present day.
    Now I deny
    This general cry;
And will proceed to tell you why
I've long since come to the conclusion,
'Tis all a popular delusion.

I have seen many a wild-beast show,
From the day when Messrs. Pidcock and Co.
Were what vulgar people call all-the-go,
To the time when society mourned for the
    loss
(All felt it, but no one like poor Mr. Cross)
Of the elephant "Chuney," who went mad, 'tis
    said,

With the pressure and pain
He felt in his brain
From constantly bearing a *trunk* on his head.

And I have set eye on
That magnanimous lion,
Brave Wallace—oh, fye on
The brutes who could hie on
Fierce bull-dogs to fly on
His monarchical mane! I declare I could cry on
The bare thought, as one weeps when one goes to see
" Ion."

And lately I've been
Down to Astley's, and seen
His wonderful elephants act; what they mean
By their actions, I've not the most distant idea;
Why they stand on their heads, why they wag their fat
  tails,
Are to me hidden mysteries, " very like whales,"
As Hamlet remarks of some cloud he is certain
He perceives up aloft, whence they let down the
  curtain,
And whither they draw up the fairies and goddesses,
With their pretty pink legs and inadequate bodices.

GATHERED LEAVES.

But of all the beasts I ever did see,
Whether of low or high degree,
    Despite the " schoolmaster,"
    And " going a-head faster,"
    The arts and the sciences,
    And all their appliances,
Never an animal, chain'd or loose,
    As yet have I heard
    Utter one single word,
Or so much as attempt to say " Bo! " to a goose.

But you'll see, if you read the next two or three pages,
That in what people now-a-days term the dark ages,
When the world was some thousand years younger or so,
Beasts could talk very well; and it wasn't thought low
For a real live monarch his prowess to brag on,
And bandy high words with an insolent dragon.

GATHERED LEAVES.

Ye Right Ancient Ballad.

HE good King Tidrich rode from Bern*
(And a funny name had he),
His charger was bay, and he took his way
　Under the greenwood-tree;
And ever he sang, as he rode along,
　" 'Tis a very fine thing
　To be a crown'd king,
And to feel one's right arm strong."

King Tidrich was clad in armour of proof
(Whatever that may be),
And his helmet shone with many a stone,
　Inserted cunningly;
While on his shield one might behold
　A lion trying
　To set off flying,
Emblazon'd in burnish'd gold.

---

* King Tidrich, Dietrich, or Theoderic, the son of Thietmar, king of Bern, and the fair Odilia, daughter of Essung Jarl, was, as it were, the central hero of that well-known, popular, and interesting work, the "Book of Heroes," which relates the deeds of the champions who attached themselves to him, and the manner in which they joined his fellowship.

GATHERED LEAVES.

King Tidrich was counting his money o'er,
   As he rode the greenwood through,
When he was aware of a "shocking affair,"
   And a terrible "to-do:"

Then loudly he shouted with pure delight,
   "A glorious row,
   I make mine avow;
I'll on, and view the fight."

GATHERED LEAVES.

And a fearful sight it was, I ween,
   As ever a king did see,
For a dragon old, and a lion bold,
   Were striving wrathfully;
But the monarch perceived from the very first—
     And it made him sad,
     For "a reason he had"—
That the lion would get the worst.

When the lion saw the royal Knight,
   These were the words he said:
"O mighty King, assistance bring,
   Or I am fairly sped;
For the battle has been both fierce and long;
     Two days and a night
     Have I urged the fight,
But the dragon's unpleasantly strong."

In a kind of Low Dutch did the lion speak,
   Nor his stops did he neglect,
But e'en in his hurry, for Lindley Murray
   Preserved a marked respect;
And he managed his H's according to rule:
     Full well I ween
     Must the beast have been
Taught at some Public School.

GATHERED LEAVES.

Long paused the royal hero then,
    Grave thoughts pass'd through his brain;
Of his queen thought he, and his fair countrie*
    He never might see again;
He thought of his warriors, that princely band,
      Of Eckhart true,
      And Helmschrot too,
And Wolfort's red right hand.†

But he thought of the lion he bore on his shield,
    And he mann'd his noble breast,—
" 'Twixt the lion and me there is sympathy,
    And a dragon I detest;
I must not see the lion slain;
      Both kings are we,
      In our degree,
I of the city and he of the plain."

The first stroke that the monarch made,
    His weapon tasted blood;
From many a scale of the dragon's mail
    Pour'd forth the crimson flood.

---

* Tidrich of Bern was also king of Aumlungaland (Italy); he espoused Herraud, daughter of King Drusiad, a relation of Attila.

† These three champions were among the eleven heroes who accompanied Tidrich in his memorable expedition to contend against the twelve guardians of the Garden of Roses at Worms.

But when the hero struck again,
    The treacherous sword
    Forsook its lord,
And brake in pieces twain.

The dragon laid him on her back
    With a triumphant air,
And flung the horse her jaws across,
    As a greyhound would seize a hare.
At a fearful pace to her rocky den,
    To serve as food
    For her young brood
Away she bore them then.

They were a charming family,
    Eleven little frights,
With deep surprise in their light green eyes,
    And fearful appetites;
And they wagg'd their tales with extreme delight,
    For to dine on king
    Is a dainty thing
When one usually dines on Knight.

Before them then the steed she threw,
    Saddle, and bridle, and crupper,
And bade them crunch its bones for lunch,
    While they saved the king for supper;

GATHERED LEAVES.

Saying, she must sleep ere she could sup,
    For after the fight
    With the lion and knight,
She was thoroughly used-up.

A lucky chance for Tidrich:
    He sought the dark cave over,
And soon the King did Adelring,*
    That famous sword discover:
"And was it here that Siegfried died? †
    That champion brave,
    Was this his grave?"
In grief the monarch cried.

"I have ridden with him in princely hosts,
    I have feasted with him in hall;
Sword, you and I will do or die,
    But we'll avenge his fall."

---

* They had a weakness for naming swords in those days, just as in the nineteenth century we delight in bestowing euphonious titles on "villa residences," puppy dogs, and men-of-war.

† Sigurd, or Siegfried, son of Sigmond, king of Netherland, is the chief hero of the Nibelungen Lay. There are various accounts of his death; one of the least improbable supposes him to have been destroyed by a dragon.

GATHERED LEAVES.

Against the cavern's rocky side
    The king essay'd
    The trusty blade,
Till the flames gleam'd far and wide.

Up rose a youthful dragon then,
  Right pallid was his hue;
For with fear and ire he view'd the fire
  From out the rock that flew.
These words he to the king did say:
    "If the noise thou dost make
    Should our mother awake,
It is thou wilt rue the day."

"Be silent, thou young viper,"
  'Twas thus the king replied,
"Thy mother slew Siegfried the true,
  A hero brave and tried;
And vengeance have I vow'd to take
    Upon ye all,
    Both great and small,
For that dear warrior's sake."

Then he aroused the dragon old,
  Attacked her with his sword,
And a fearful fight, with strength and might,
  Fought he, that noble lord.

GATHERED LEAVES.

The dragon's fiery breath, I ween,
    Made his cuirass stout
    Red hot throughout:
Such a sight was never seen.

Despair lent strength to the monarch then;
    A mighty stroke he made,
Through the dragon's neck, without a check,
    He passed his trenchant blade.
At their mother's fall, each little fright
    Began to yell
    Like an imp of hell,
And nearly stunn'd the knight.

He struck right and left with Adelring,
    That trusty sword and good,
And in pieces small chopp'd each and all
    Of the dragon's hateful brood.
King Tidrich thus at honour's call,
    On German Land,
    With his strong right hand,
Avenged bold Siegfried's fall.

Now ye whose spirits thrill to hear
    The trumpet-voice of fame,
Or love to read of warrior deed,
    Remember Tidrich's name;

GATHERED LEAVES.

And mourn that the days of chivalry
  Are past and o'er,
  And live no more,
Save in their glorious memory.

Yet when Prince Albert rides abroad,
  Our gracious Queen may feel
As well content, as if he went,
  Encased in plates of steel;
Relying on the new Police,
  Those bulwarks of the state,
That on their beat, no dragons eat
  The Prince off his own plate!

[Should any reader wish to learn more of the various personages here mentioned, we refer him to the " Illustrations of Northern Antiquities, from the earlier Teutonic and Scandinavian Romances," to which we are indebted for our information on the subject.]

THE ENCHANTED NET.

OULD we only give credit to half we are told,
There were sundry strange monsters existing
of old;

As evinced 'on the *ex pede Herculem* plan,
Which from merely a footstep presumes the whole man,

By our *Savans* disturbing those very large bones,
Which have turn'd (for the rhyme's sake, perhaps) into stones,
      And have chosen to wait a
      Long while hid in *strata*,
While old Time has been dining on empires and thrones.
      Old bones and dry bones,
      Leg-bones and thigh-bones,
Bones of the vertebræ, bones of the tail,—
Very like, only more so, the bones of a whale;
Bones that were very long, bones that were very short
(They have never as yet found a real fossil merry-thought;
Perchance because mastodons, burly and big,
Consider'd all funny-bones quite *infra dig.*);
Skulls have they found in strange places embedded,
Which, at least, prove their owners were very long-headed;
And other queer things,—which 'tis not my intention,
Lest I weary your patience, at present to mention,—
As I think I can prove, without further apology,
What I said to be true, sans appeal to geology,
That there lived in the good old days gone by
Things unknown to our modern philosophy,
And a giant was then no more out of the way
Than a dwarf is now in the present day.

GATHERED LEAVES.

Sir Eppo of Epstein was young, brave, and fair;
Dark were the curls of his clustering hair,
Dark the moustache that o'ershadow'd his lip,
And his glance was as keen as the sword at his hip;
Tho' the enemy's charge was like lightning's fierce shock,
His seat was as firm as the wave-beaten rock;
And woe to the foeman, whom pride or mischance
Opposed to the stroke of his conquering lance.
He carved at the board, and he danced in the hall,
And the ladies admired him, each one and all.
In a word, I should say, he appears to have been
As nice a young "ritter" as ever was seen.

    He could not read nor write,
    He could not spell his name,

    Towards being a clerk, Sir Eppo, his (†) mark,
    Was as near as ever he came.

GATHERED LEAVES.

    He had felt no vexation
    From multiplication;
    Never puzzled was he
    By the rule of three;
    The practice he'd had
    Did not drive him mad,
    Because it all lay
    Quite a different way.
  The Asses' Bridge, that Bridge of Sighs,
  Had (lucky dog!) ne'er met his eyes.
In a very few words he express'd his intention
Once for all to decline every Latin declension,
When persuaded to add, by the good Father Herman,
That most classical tongue to his own native German.
    And no doubt he was right in
    Point of fact, for a knight in
Those days was supposed to like nothing but fighting;
And one who had learn'd any language that is hard
Would have stood a good chance of being burn'd for a wizard.
Education being then never push'd to the verge ye
Now see it, was chiefly confined to the clergy.

'Twas a southerly wind and a cloudy sky,
For aught that I know to the contrary;
If it wasn't, it ought to have been proper*ly*,

GATHERED LEAVES.

As it's certain Sir Eppo, his feather bed scorning,
Thought that *something* proclaim'd it a fine hunting
    morning;
      So, pronouncing his benison
      O'er a cold haunch of venison,
He floor'd the best half, drank a gallon of beer,
And set out on the Taurus to chase the wild deer.

Sir Eppo he rode through the good greenwood,
And his bolts flew fast and free;
He knock'd over a hare, and he passed the lair
(The tenant was out) of a grisly bear;
He started a wolf, and he got a snap shot
At a bounding roe, but he touched it not,
Which caused him to mutter a naughty word
In German, which luckily nobody heard,
For he said it right viciously;
And he struck his steed with his armed heel,
As though horse-flesh were tougher than iron or steel,
Or anything else that's unable to feel.

What is the sound that meets his ear?
Is it the plaint of some wounded deer?
Is it the wild-fowl's mournful cry,
Or the scream of yon eagle soaring high?

Or is it only the southern breeze
As it sighs through the boughs of the dark pine trees?
No, Sir Eppo, be sure 'tis not any of these:
    And hark, again!
    It comes more plain—
'Tis a woman's voice in grief or pain.

    Like an arrow from the string,
    Like a stone that leaves the sling,
Like a railroad-train with a queen inside,
With directors to poke and directors to guide,
Like the rush upon deck when a vessel is sinking,
Like (I vow I'm hard up for a simile) winking!
In less time than by name you Jack Robinson can call,
Sir Eppo dash'd forward o'er hedge, ditch, and hollow,
In a steeple-chase style I'd be sorry to follow,
And found a young lady chain'd up by the ankle—
Yes, chain'd up in a cool and business-like way,
As if she'd been only the little dog Tray;
While, the more to secure any knight-errant's pity,
She was really and truly excessively pretty.

Here was a terrible state of things!
Down from his saddle Sir Eppo springs,

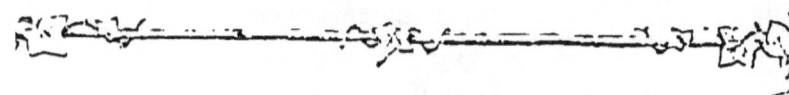

GATHERED LEAVES.

As lightly as if he were furnish'd with wings,
While every plate in his armour rings.
The words that he utter'd were short and few,
But pretty much to the purpose too,
As sternly he asked, with lowering brow,
" Who's been and done it, and where is he now?"

   'Twere long to tell
   Each word that fell
From the coral lips of that demoiselle;
However, as far as I'm able to see,
The pith of the matter appear'd to be
That a horrible giant, twelve feet high,
Having gazed on her charms with a covetous eye,
Had storm'd their castle, murder'd papa,
Behaved very rudely to poor dear mamma,
Walk'd off with the family jewels and plate,
And the tin and herself at a terrible rate;
   Then by way of conclusion
   To all this confusion,
   Tied her up like a dog
   To a nasty great log,
To induce her (the brute) to become Mrs. Gog;
That 'twas not the least use for Sir Eppo to try
To chop off his head, or to poke out his eye,

GATHERED LEAVES

As he'd early in life done a bit of Achilles
(Which, far better than taking an "Old Parr's life-
pill" is),
Had been dipp'd in the Styx, or some equally old
stream,
And might now face unharm'd a battalion of Cold-
stream.

But she'd thought of a scheme
Which did certainly seem
Very likely to pay—no mere vision or dream :—
It appears that the giant each day took a nap
For an hour (the wretch!) with his head in her lap :
Oh, she hated it so! but then what could she do?
Here she paused, and Sir Eppo remark'd, " Very true ;"
And that during this time one might pinch, punch, or
shake him,
Or do just what one pleased, but that nothing could
wake him,
While each horse and each man in the emperor's pay
Would not be sufficient to move him away,
Without magical aid, from the spot where he lay.
In an old oak chest, in an up-stairs room
Of poor papa's castle, was kept an heir-loom,
An enchanted net, made of iron links,
Which was brought from Palestine, she thinks,

GATHERED LEAVES.

By her great grandpapa, who had been a Crusader;
If she had but got that, she was sure it would aid her.
    Sir Eppo, kind man,
      Approves of the plan;
Says he'll do all she wishes as quick as he can;
Begs she wont fret if the time should seem long;
Snatches a kiss, which was "pleasant but wrong;"
Mounts, and taking a fence in good fox-hunting style,
Sets off for her family-seat on the Weil.

    The sun went down,
    The bright stars burn'd,
    The morning came,
    And the knight return'd;
    The net he spread
    O'er the giant's bed,
While Eglantine, and Hare-bell blue,
And some nice green moss on the spot he threw;
Lest perchance the monster alarm should take,
And not choose to sleep from being too *wide awake*.
    Hark to that sound!
    The rocks around
    Tremble—it shakes the very ground;
    While Irmengard cries,
    As tears stream from her eyes,—
A lady-like weakness we must not despise—

(And here, let me add, I have been much to blame,
As I long ago ought to have mention'd her name):
"Here he comes! now do hide yourself, dear Eppo,
    pray;
For *my* sake, I entreat you, keep out of his way."
            Scarce had the knight
            Time to get out of sight
Among some thick bushes, which cover'd him quite,
Ere the giant appear'd. Oh! he was such a fright!
He was very square built, a good twelve feet in
    height,
And his waistcoat (three yards round the waist) seem'd
    too tight;
While, to add even yet to all this singularity,
He had but one eye, and his whiskers were carroty.

What an anxious moment! Will he lie down?
Ah, how their hearts beat! he seems to frown,—
No; 'tis only an impudent fly that's been teasing
His *snub*lime proboscis, and set him a sneezing.
            Attish hu! attish hu!
            You brute, how I wish you
        Were but as genteel as the Irish lady,
            Dear Mrs. O'Grady,
Who, chancing to sneeze in a noble duke's face,
Hoped she hadn't been guilty of splashing his Grace.

GATHERED LEAVES.

Now, look out. Yes, he will! No, he won't! By
    the powers!
I thought he was taking alarm at the flowers;
But it luckily seems, his gigantic invention
Has at once set them down as a little attention
On Irmengard's part,—done by way of suggestion
That she means to say "Yes," when he next pops the
    question.

There! he's down! now he yawns, and in one minute
    more—
I thought so, he's safe—he's beginning to snore;
He is wrapp'd in that sleep he shall wake from no
    more.
From his girdle the knight takes a ponderous key;
It fits—and once more is fair Irmengard free.

From heel to head, and from head to heel,
They wrap their prey in that net of steel,
And they *croché* the edges together with care,
As you finish a purse for a fancy-fair,
Till the last knot is tied by the diligent pair.
At length they have ended their business laborious,
And Eppo shouts, "Bagg'd him, by all that is
    glorious!"

GATHERED LEAVES.

No billing and cooing,
You must up and be doing.
Depend on't, Sir Knight, this is no time for wooing;
You'll discover, unless you progress rather smarter,
That catching a giant's like catching a Tartar:
He still has some thirty-five minutes to sleep.
Close to this spot hangs a precipice steep,
Like Shakspeare's tall cliff which they show one at
    Dover;
Drag him down to the brink, and then let him roll over;
As they scarce make a capital crime of infanticide,
There can't be any harm in a little giganticide.

" Pull him, and haul him! take care of his head!
Oh, how my arms ache—he's as heavy as lead!
That'll do, love—I'm sure I can move him alone,
Though I'm certain the brute weighs a good forty stone.
Yo! heave ho! roll him along
(It's exceedingly lucky the net's pretty strong);
Once more—that's it—there, now, I think
He's done to a turn, he rests on the brink;
At it again, and over he goes
To furnish a feast for the hooded crows;
Each vulture that makes the Taurus his home
May dine upon giant for months to come."

GATHERED LEAVES.

Lives there a man so thick of head
To whom it must in words be said,
How Eppo did the lady wed,
And built upon the giant's bed

A castle, wall'd and turreted?
We will hope not; or if there be,
Defend us from his company!

A FYTTE OF THE BLUES.

(*Air*—"THE OLD ENGLISH GENTLEMAN.")

F Woman's rights and Woman's wrongs we've
    heard much talk of late,
The first seem most extensive, and the latter
    very great;
And Mrs. Ellis warns men, not themselves to agitate,
For 'neath petticoats and pinafores is hid the future fate
Of this wondrous nineteenth century, the youngest
    child of Time!

The Turks they had a notion, fit alone for Turks and
    fools,
That womankind has no more mind than horses or than
    mules;
But this idea's exploded quite, as to your cost you'll
    find,
If you intend to change or bend some stalwart female
    mind,
In this Amazonian century, precocious child of Time.

GATHERED LEAVES.

If by external signs you seek this strength of mind to trace,
You'll observe a very "powerful" expression in her face;
The lady's stockings will be blue, and inky be her hand,
And her head quite full of something hard she doesn't understand,
    Like a puzzle-pated Bluestocking, one of the modern time.

And her dress will be peculiar both in fabric and in make,
An artistic classic tragic highly-talented mistake;
Which is what she calls " effective," though I'd rather not express
The effect produced on thoughtless minds by such a style of dress,
    When worn by some awful Bluestocking, one of the modern time.

She'll talk about statistics, and ask if you're inclined
To join the progress movement for development of mind.
If you inquire what that means, she'll frown and say 'tis best
Such matter should be understood, but never be express'd,
    By a stern suggestive Bluestocking, in this mystic modern time.

GATHERED LEAVES.

She'll converse upon æsthetics, and then refer to figures,
And turn from Angels bright and fair to sympathise with Niggers,

Whom she'll style " our sable brethren," and pretend are martyrs quite ;
And with Mrs. H—t B—r St—e, she'll swear that black is white,
   Like a trans-Atlantic Bluestocking, one of the modern time.

GATHERED LEAVES.

She never makes a pudding, and she never makes a
    shirt,
And if she's got some little blues, they're black and
    blue with dirt;
When the wretched man her husband comes, though
    tired he may be,
She'll regenerate society instead of making tea,
  Like a real strong-minded Bluestocking, the plague
    of the modern time.

MORAL.

The moral of my song is this, just leave all "ics" and
    "ologies"
For men to exercise their brains, on platforms and in
    colleges;
Let woman's proud and honour'd place be still the
    fireside,
And still man's household deities, his mother and his
    bride,
  In this our nineteenth century, the favour'd child of
    Time.

THE FORFEIT HAND;

A LEGEND OF BRABANT.*

Fytte ye First.

ERALDUS the Abbot sat bolt upright,
Bolt upright, in his great arm-chair,
He ground his teeth, and his beard beneath,
    Seemed *crêpé* with anger every hair;
And every hair, whether grizzled or white,
On his head stood erect (as so often the case is,
Whene'er fury or fear better feeling effaces),
Thus encircling his tonsure, which same a smooth space is
In the desert of scalp a monastic oasis!

Geraldus the Abbot his temper had lost,
    Insult had fall'n on the Prelate proud—
Heretic hands in a blanket had tost
    Lay Brother Ludwig, one of the crowd

---

* The facts (?) of this Legend are taken, by poetical license, from "Legends of the Rhine," by the author of "Highways and Byways."

GATHERED LEAVES.

Of the Abbot's dependants, a useful and able man,
Neither fish, flesh, nor fowl, half a friar, half stable-
    man.
But this shaking his brain so completely had addled,
That the next time Geraldus's palfrey he saddled,
He forgot both the girths—an important omission,
Which occasion'd a sudden and rude imposition
On our general Mamma: (we allude to the Earth,
Who most kindly supports us, who gave our race
        birth,
And will give, when breath fails, and we cannot re-
    place it,
Furnish'd lodgings, a stone, and the motto, "*Hic jacet.*")

"*Hic*" did "*jacet*" Geraldus, when rashly he tried,
Foot in stirrup, to climb to his saddle and ride;
        For the saddle turn'd round,
        And he came to the ground,
With a hollow and pectoral "*woughf*" kind of sound.
        (Printing cannot express it,
        But 'twill help you to guess it,
If you've ever remark'd the peculiar behaviour,
When he rams a large stone, of an Irish pavier.)
        Well, he wasn't much hurt,
        But appear'd from the dirt,

GATHERED LEAVES.

Which adhered to his mitre and robes, to be rather
A ghastly and horrible sight for a Father
Confessor, who ere he thus rudely was tost
In the mire, was got up regardless of cost.

For this fall he vow'd vengeance, and straightway on
  that theme a
Writ was prepared which wound up with "Anathema!"

GATHERED LEAVES.

Yolenta of Corteryke sat in her bower,
    Which was not an arbour
    Where earwigs might harbour,
And availing themselves of some *al fresco* tea-table,
Lie and kick on their backs amidst everything
    eatable,
But the very best room in the very best tower.
    Yolenta was young and Yolenta was fair,
      She'd extremely pink cheeks and extremely smooth
        hair,
And a pair of bright eyes with so roguish a glance in 'em,
That the spirit of mischief and fun seem'd to dance in
    'em;
And a sweet little foot and a dear little hand,
And a thorough-bred air, and a look of command,
As noble a lady as one in the land.

Yet Yolenta had "suffer'd;"—her little affairs
Of the heart had gone roughly, a custom of theirs
From time immemorial, since Helen lost Troy,
And pious Æneas made Dido a toy
Of the moment, then left her, a striking variety,
In the uniform course of his orthodox piety.
A young gent was her first love, of birth and condi-
    tion,
Whose very name, Loridon, seem'd an admission

GATHERED LEAVES.

He was form'd to adore, but then what's in a name?
Had they christen'd him Jack, she'd have "loved him
    the same,"
Because—mark the reason—her Pa had been rude
To his Guv'nor, which led to a family feud.
So the Lord Lettelhausen called up his son Loridon,
And exclaim'd, "Of all girls, to have fixed on that
    horrid one!
The daughter, you scamp, of the man I detest!
But I'll never consent! if I do, I'll be—blest!
Miss Yolenta, indeed! why, my garters and stars!
This is worse than your tricks with latch-keys and
    cigars!
Now, be off to the wars, nor on any pretences,
Show your face here again till you've come to your
    senses."
    So *Malbrook se va-t-en guerre,*
    In a state of deep despair.

Then Yolenta's papa thought he'd best take a part in it,
By performing the *rôle* of the tyrant and martinet,
    And proposed as a suitor,
    An old coadjutor
    In many a dark deed, which no one but a brute or
Barbarian would perpetrate, one Baron Corteryke,
Whom he coolly inform'd her she certainly ought to like,

GATHERED LEAVES.

But, whether or no, in a week's time must marry—
    And his will being the law,
    This mediæval Bashaw
Pooh-pooh'd Ma'mselle's suggestion of wishing to tarry,
And so, sending to Gunter, got up, like John Parry,
A first-rate entertainment, and vast charivari;
But yet, after all, was unable to carry
Out his cruel intentions, for 'twixt cup and lip
There occurr'd in this case a most notable slip;
To describe it, our metre we've stol'n, 'twill be seen,
From the song of one "Jock," who's sirnamed Hazeldean.

    " The kirk was deckt at Eventide,
        The tapers glimmer'd fair,
        The Baron Cort'ryke sought his bride,
        And this time she *was* there!
    She said, ' I will,' as if a pill
        Had stuck within her throat,
    But fortune kind was still inclined
        To grant an antidote;

    " For scarce beside the altar stone,
        The nuptial knot was tied,
    When some vile party, name unknown,
        Stabb'd Cort'ryke in the side!

GATHERED LEAVES.

His anguish sore, not long he bore,
Physicians wor in vain,
Death did consider him and his widder,
And eased him of his pain."

So the lovely Yolenta was "quit for the fright,"
Took the name, tin, and castle (a rare widow's mite),
And wonder'd how Loridon fared in the fight.

"It was Geraldus' serving man,
Ludwigus he was hight,
For fair Bettye, that damsel free,
He sigh'd both day and night;
Fair Bettye at the tapestry wrought,
In Dame Yolenta's bower;
To ease the pain of this her swain,
She lack'd both will and power.

"Dan Cupid, that mischievous boy,
Ludwig to sorrow brought;
For ogling of the fair Bettye,
Him, Dame Yolenta caught;
And as in true love men are still
(As well as oysters) cross'd,
Ludwig, to cure his fantasy,
Was in a blanket toss'd."

"*Hinc illæ lachrymæ,*" thence all these woes!
From this pitching and tossing the shindy arose!

'Tis the voice of a herald! I heard him proclaim,
That he carries a summons for Corteryke's dame,
  Which sets forth how that same
  Fair lady's to blame,
For the high misdemeanour, the sin, and the shame,
Of tossing a lay brother, Ludwig by name,
In a blanket, whereby she did cut, wound, and
   maim,
And maliciously injure, and wilfully lame,
And despitefully maltreat, deride, and make game,
And confuse, and abuse, and misuse, and defame!
  A monk of Saint Benedict,
  Which by a then edict
Was a legal offence; so Yolenta was cited
  To appear, and show cause
  Why she'd broken the laws,
At the next petty sessions, where she was invited
To plead in her own proper person, and wait a
Decree from my Lord Lettelhausen, the pater
Of poor banish'd Loridon, likewise the frater
Of the plaintiff Geraldus, an excellent hater
Of all who opposed him, a reg'lar first-rater,
Full of envy and malice, a real aggravator,

Who'd have charmed Doctor Johnson, that learn'd commentator,
Had he chanced but to live a few centuries later.

The herald he stood in the castle hall,
    Seneschal, warder, and page, were there;
And he read his citation fair and free,
In a baritone voice that went up to G,
    As loudly as he could bawl.
And he clear'd his throat, and he push'd back his hair
With a negligent, nonchalant, jaunty air;
As though he would ask of the bystanding "parties,"—
" Pri'thee, what do ye think of *me*, my hearties?"

Yolenta she smiled, and Yolenta she frown'd,
And her delicate foot in a pet tapp'd the ground;
And when she turn'd to the herald to greet him,
The flash of her eye seem'd to say she could eat him;
Though their points curl'd up to the knees of his trews,
I'd have been sorry to stand in his shoes.
Then she answer'd him shortly and sweetly,—
    " You're a bold man, Sir Herald, I trow—
A bold and an insolent man I ween;
    A scurrilous knave, I make mine avow;
But perhaps you may find that I'm not quite so green
As your masters imagine. You've done it most featly

GATHERED LEAVES.

This time I'll allow;
But it struck me just now,
When you entered my castle to kick up this row,
You'd have fared quite as well if you'd journey'd on
    farther:
I'm afraid you've, young man, put your foot in it—
    rather!"
Then she sign'd with her hand, and six mutes in black
    armour,

As by magic appear'd, laid their lances in rest,
And directed their points to the herald's bare breast,—

A sight which it must be confess'd might alarm a
Brave man in those very unscrupulous days,
When a life, more or less, was a mere bagatelle;
And when sticking a porker, or stabbing a swell,
Were alike household duties—a singular phase
In those "sweet" Middle Ages, on which such depen-
    dence is
Placed by young ladies with "Puseyite" tendencies.
          Howe'er this may be,
          Our herald felt he
Had no call to assist in this *felo de se;*
So straight fell on his knee,
And exclaim'd, "Don't you see,
Noble Countess Yolenta, this good jest at present
Is a great deal too pointed and sharp to be pleasant?
          I humbly beg pardon,
          So pray don't be hard on
A penitent cove, whose name's printed this card on."
Then he handed his pasteboard, gilt type, and a border,
Stamped,

> De Rodon.
> Heraldic work furnished to order.

GATHERED LEAVES

Yolenta she smiled, and Yolenta she frown'd,
Then light rang her laugh with its silvery sound.
"Rise, valiant De Rodon," she mockingly cried,
"And behold by what foemen your mettle's been tried."
Then each sable spearsman his vizor unclasps,
And six laughing girls with bright mischievous eyes,
Poke their fun at De Rodon, who's mute with surprise
And disgust, while Yolenta her riding wand grasps,
Sharply switches the recreant kneeling before her,
    And turns to depart,—
    When up with a start
Springs De Rodon, and pallid with anger leans o'er
    her.
Then hisses these words in her ear,—"Ere you smile
Or rejoice in your stratagem, listen awhile,
And learn that a herald discharging his duty
Is sacred; despite of your wealth, rank, and beauty,
For the stroke you have dealt me YOUR FAIR HAND IS
    FORFEIT;
By the axe of the headsman, ere many days, off it
Shall be hewn, and when next men to fury you goad
    on,
Bear in mind the revenge of the herald De Rodon!"

GATHERED LEAVES.

Fytte ye Second.

WHEN the weather is hazy, and not the least
        sign in,
The clouds of their showing a silvery lining;
When a bill's coming due, and you've no
    chance of meeting it;
When old Harry's to pay, and the pitch has no heat
    in it;
When you're thinking of popping, and suddenly find
That your inamorata's not that way inclined;
When you've publish'd a novel, and find it don't sell;
When you rise from the wine cup, and don't feel quite
    well;
When some six-feet-six monster, by jealousy led,
Suggests "satisfaction" or "punching your head;"
When your wife's taken cross, or the "olive-branch" sick,
When your wardrobe's worn out, and your tailor won't
    "tick;"
When your money's all gone, and your creditors dun
    for it;
      I think you'll agree,
      That the best plan will be
To (I speak in the language of slang) "cut and run
    for it."

Thus, then, reason'd Yolenta of Corteryke, but
With this difference, she "ran" to avoid the "cut"
Of all cuts "most unkindest" (bad grammar, you
    know,
When it's written by Shakespeare no longer is so),
Which De Rodon had promised her, *axe*-ing her hand,
In a manner no woman of feeling could stand
With composure; so straightway Yolenta resolved
To make herself scarce, which manœuvre involved
Much domestic confusion; each man and each maid
Requiring their wages, and board-wages, paid
For a month in advance; while the butler grew crusty
As his oldest port wine; and fair Bettye cried "Must I
Be the cause of this woe—from my dear mistress sever—
Lose my place and my perquisites! which my endeavour
Has still been to draw mild. Well, I never did—never!"
(Then addressing the public at large) "Did *you* ever?"
These arrangements concluded, Yolenta began
Packing up—the last duty of travelling man—
    But the business of life
      To maid, widow, or wife,
Except Ida Pfeiffer, that wonder, who can
With umbrella and tooth-brush, reach far Yucatan,
    And, like Ariel, span
The earth with a girdle, which some commentator
On Shakespeare imagines must mean the Equator.

GATHERED LEAVES.

Well, she packed up her traps in a leathern valise,
Which contain'd sundry stockings, a nice new ——,
    but he's

No gentleman, clearly, who'd, Hobbs-like, the locks
Endeavour to pick of *so* private a box.
Then, by way of disguise, Dame Yolenta decided
Don't be horrified, dear lady-readers, though I did

Myself think it strange that my heroine chose
To set out on her rambles attired in *such* clothes,
For convenience of trav'lling, perhaps, to assume a
Man's dress—not the epicene compromise, Bloomer,
But the regular masculine *propria quæ maribus*,
A male coat, a male waistcoat, *et ceteris paribus*,
    A gay cap and feather,
    Unfit for bad weather,—
A sword by her side, and a fine prancing horse,
Which she sat, I'm afraid, not "aside" but "across;"
    With one groom to attend her—
    Nought else to defend her—
Like a "Young Lochinvar" of the feminine gender,
The ill-fated Yolenta rode off at a canter,
And became what the stockbrokers term "a levanter."

    Now you'll please to suppose,
    That she follow'd her nose,
A fine aquiline organ that proudly arose,
    Filling just the right space
    On her bright sparkling face,
Excelling, as butterfly's better than grub,
Those unlucky "*retroussés*," in *plain* English,
    "snub,"
Which men always pretend to, and often desire,
But never can really and truly admire;

GATHERED LEAVES.

      She follow'd her nose
      To (I blush to disclose
For it *does* seem so forward; but then no one knows
The whys and the wherefores, the *cons* and the *pros*,
Which decide other folks; in the fair sex our trust is
Extreme; so we'll strive not to do her injustice.)
For some reason unknown, then, she follow'd her nose
To the camp of King Charles, in which Loridon chose
To wear out his exile, and solace his woes,
By assisting that monarch to conquer his foes.

      It were long to relate
      All the evils that Fate
Seem'd resolved to pour down on our heroine's pate;
      How, on reaching the camp,
      She was told that a scamp
Of a *Douanier*, at the last town she quitted,
      Had, as usual, omitted
To see that her passport was legally *visé'd;*
Although, when she handed his fees to him, he said
      It was all right and proper
      And no one would stop her;
Which was false, for it quickly appear'd by the law
Of the strong, she was somebody's prisoner of war;
Next, for fear in her wrath she a breach of the peace
Should commit, or attempt to assault the police,

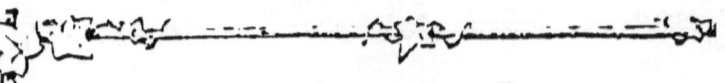

GATHERED LEAVES.

They disarm'd her—laid hands on her watch, chain,
    and seal
All the very best gold, and the watch not much
    thicker
Than a mod'rate sized turnip—no end of a ticker),
    And hurried her off to the then Pentonville
Model Prison, to wait, all forlorn and alone,
And to "carve her name on the Newgate stone,"
Till this terrible somebody's pleasure was known.

The unpleasant unknown was one Giles de Laval,
A marshal of France, and a very great " pal "
   (Or paladin rather) of King Charles *le Beau,*
      (Or "*le Gros,*" or "*le Sot,*"
      Which, I really don't know ;
But 'twas one of the three, for there's no nation
    showers
Such peculiar nicknames on its "governing powers"
   As our trusty ally Monsieur Johnny Crapaud) ;
This same Giles de Laval, then, who ruled the French
    host,
And the roast, and the coast, made the most of his post ;
      Dealt just as he chose
      With his friends and his foes,
And was as autocratic, and nearly as fickle as,
That bugbear of Europe, a certain Czar Nicholas—

GATHERED LEAVES.

This identical Giles, for some reason he had,
Seem'd resolved that Yolenta should "go to the bad:"
    (He possess'd such sharp eyes
    They pierced through her disguise
At first sight, to her terror and shame and surprise),
So he scolded her well, wouldn't hear her confessions,
But return'd her, to answer for all her transgressions,
To Geraldus, in time for the next quarter sessions.

Unhappy Yolenta! Geraldus confined her
In a dungeon, deep, damp, and unpleasant; behind her
Was a ring in the wall, and some rusty old chains,
And there lay in one corner a skull void of brains,
And a horrid leg-bone stood upright in another,
Which must once have belong'd to "a man and a
    brother;"
Then a sturdy support, now a most "unreal mockery,"
A relic suggestively placed there to shock her eye,
And bid her prepare for the doom that awaited her,—
    For her dinner they brought her,
    Dry bread and cold water,
Wretched food, and by no means enlivening drink
(Whatever hydraulic George Cruikshank may think
To the contrary), then, lest they'd not aggravated her
By this treatment, enough, the brutes next dissipated
    her

GATHERED LEAVES.

Last agreeable illusion: a letter was given her,
Sign'd and seal'd by some friendly (?) anonymous
    scrivener,
Short, not sweet, for the missive consisted of one
Line, "*The Lord Lettelhausen's no longer a son*,"—
    From which pleasant allusion,
    She reach'd the conclusion,
That, by some vicious dodge, which she could not dis-
    cover
De Laval had "used up" and expended her lover.

Unhappy Yolenta! forsaken, heart-broken,
She drew from her bosom a cherish'd love-token;
A dark curling lock of her Loridon's hair,
Fix'd her eyes on it, shed o'er it tears of despair,
Then devour'd it with kisses, and dropp'd on her knees,
To implore with deep fervour that Heaven would please
Pardon Loridon's sins, forgive hers, and so let her
Rejoin, and remain with, one whom she loved better
Far than life; then o'ercome by conflicting emotions,
A fainting fit ended her tears and devotions.

GATHERED LEAVES.

Ye Last Scene of All.

APING and yawning,
  Their feather-beds scorning,
  All the burghers of Ghent rose betimes in
    the morning,
    For a " shocking event "
    Was to take place in Ghent,
And the public delighted in hangings and quarterings,
Mutilations and tortures, and such kind of slaughterings,
Just as much as an Anglican crowd in the present day,
Think attending the " Manning " *finale* a pleasant day ;
    So extremely they bustled,
      Pushed, jostled, and hustled,
Climb'd up lamp-posts (there were none!), on each
    rising ground
Stood to view the procession, as slowly it wound
Its way to the cathedral, where, at the high altar
    The condemn'd was "*pro se*"
      To appear, or else be
Declared recusant, most contumacious, defaulter,
Et cetera, et cetera, in fact, all the " bosh "
That the law could devise, horrid stuff which won't wash,
And yet seems to last pretty well through all ages,
Keeps solicitors going, and provides their clerks wages.

GATHERED LEAVES.

'Twas a splendid and beautiful pageant, that same;
First a body of archers and shield-bearers came;
Then some dear little choristers, dressed all in white,
Who each carried a *chandelle bénie*, or " child's light,"
Which being bless'd by the Pope, it appears to my thick
  head,
Must, in spite of its wick, have no longer been *wicked*;
Next came Abbot Geraldus, profusely ornate
With mitre, and crozier, and garments of state;
Then the Herald de Rodon, in great exultation,
Highly pleased with himself, and the whole "situa-
  tion;"
        Then a servitor, bearing
        A big candle, flaring
Up like mad, and creating a vast cloud of vapour,
Or smoke (which affair was a "penitent taper"),
On a silver "*Lavabo*," a word which they say,
In middle-age Latin, means simply a tray;
And after this penitent candle there came
Our penitent heroine, looking the same,
And feeling—however, I'll leave you to guess
How the poor thing would feel in so cruel a mess.
Then came something of which the description we'd
  best give
Is, like Tennyson's rhymes, it was "sweetly sug-
  gestive"—

A large shield, in the centre whereof was depicted
A hand lately severed,—the artist, addicted
('Twas De Rodon himself) to pre-Raphaelite rules,
Had made the wrist *"sanglant"* with drops from it
"gules."

Then directly behind this agreeable affair
Came the city "Jack Ketch" with his horrid axe bare!

GATHERED LEAVES.

Then more spearmen; and then rush'd the crowd out
    of breath,
With their eagerness all to be in at the death.

    Her eyes dim with despair,
    All dishevell'd her hair,
And the fair " FORFEIT HAND" with its rounded arm bare,
With brow madly throbbing, and footsteps that falter,—
The wretched Yolenta is led to the altar;
    While De Rodou proclaims,
    By his titles and names,
That the Lord Lettelhausen, Grand Seigneur, and Knight
Of some half-dozen orders, demands as his right
The forfeited hand of the culprit Yolenta.
Then Geraldus replies, " By the general consent, a
Demand thus in accordance with justice and law
Is granted. Let Lord Lettelhausen now draw
Near the altar, and take, by the Church's command,
As his right and possession, the FORFEITED HAND! "

    A stalwart arm is round her thrown,
        Fondly the forfeit hand is press'd;
    No more forsaken and alone,
        She sinks upon a manly breast.

At length the evil days are past—
Her griefs, her trials, all are over,
Long wept, long sought, regained at last,
'Tis Loridon, her own true lover.

Whose Papa having very obligingly done
The genteel thing, in dying exactly when one
Would have wish'd him, by that means enabled his son
To step into his shoes, just in time to disk*i*ver a
Mode of enacting the gallant deliverer;
  As we've tried to rehearse
  For your pleasure in verse,
If we've happen'd to fail,—and too clearly you know it,—
Bear in mind that we never set up for a poet.

THE BALLAD OF BOREÄNA.

Y brain is wearied with thy prate,
                Boreäna.
  I sit and curse my hapless fate,
                Boreäna.
What time the rain pours down the gutter,
Still your platitudes you utter,
                Boreäna.
I unholy wishes mutter,
                Boreäna.

Ere the night-light's flame was waning,
                Boreäna,
While the cats were serenading,
                Boreäna,
Sheep were bleating, oxen lowing,
We heard the beasts to Smithfield going,
                Boreäna.
You said the butcher's bill was owing,
                Boreäna.

GATHERED LEAVES.

At Cremorne we two alone,
     Boreäna,
Ere my wisdom teeth were grown,
     Boreäna,
While the dancers gaily hopp'd,
And the brass band never stopp'd,
     Boreäna,
I to thee the question popp'd,
     Boreäna.

She stood beside the area gate,
     Boreäna.
She did it just to aggravate,
     Boreäna.
She saw me wink, she heard me swear,
She recognised the scoundrel there,
     Boreäna.
She *knows* a bailiff I can't bear,
     Boreäna.

The cursed writ, he push'd it through,
     Boreäna,
The area rails, and gave it you,
     Boreäna.

GATHERED LEAVES.

The infernal summons me unnerved,
He from his duty never swerved,
      Boreäna.
On thee, my bride, the writ he served,
      Boreäna.

Oh! narrow-minded county court,
      Boreäna!
'Tis death to me, to them 'tis sport,
      Boreäna.

GATHERED LEAVES.

Oh! stab in my most tender place,
My pocket! oh, the deep disgrace,
    Boreäna!
I fell down flat upon my face,
    Boreäna.

They fined me at the court next day,
    Boreäna.
Lock'd up, how can I get away,
    Boreäna?
I don't perceive of hope a ray.
'Tis a true bill, but oh! I say,
    Boreäna,
How, without tin, am I to pay,
    Boreäna?

When turns the never-pausing mill,
    Boreäna,
I tread, I do not dare stand still,
    Boreäna.
At home, of beer thou drink'st thy fill;
I may not come to thee and swill,
    Boreäna.
I hear the rolling of the mill,
    Boreäna.

TO A PUNNING BEAUTY.

OHNSON, that pompous, ponderous pedant who
A dictionary wrote, which Pitt read through,
Declared, I've heard, and in my memory lock it,
The man who'd make a pun would pick a pocket.

Now, if the dictionarian's dictum's true,
Who'll tell us what a punning girl may do?
Some answering echo doth this news impart,
The girl who'd make a pun would steal a heart.

TO MRS. G. H. VIRTUE.

HOU better half of Virtue, gentle friend,
　Fairly to thee I, Fairlegh, greeting send ;
　Frankly I give what frankly you desire ;
　　You thus Frank Fairlegh's autograph acquire.
To make assurance doubly sure, this medley
Of Franks and Fairleghs thus I sign—

Frank Smedley

VALENTINES.

I.

IF you loves I, as I loves you,
   With an affection strong and true,
   And always as I wish you do,
   And promise not to grow up blue,
Or write "sweet things," or "Sonnets to . . ."
And never want a bonnet new
Until your pin-money is due;
And snub each " got up" puppy who
Dares to presume to flirt with you;
And sew on buttons not a few,
As " Wedded Beauty " ought to do;
I'd not mind playing Edwin to
Your Angelina! What say you?

Valentine's Eve.

II.

AVE you caught a Valentine?
Prithee, fair one, say.
If not, will you, dear, be mine
On this blessed day?
On this day when lads and lasses,
Of themselves make precious asses,
Writing sentimental verses
(Than which *I* think nothing worse is),
Raving about hearts of tinder
(Calves' hearts roasted to a cinder),
Praising up that little stupid,
Fat, untailor'd idiot, Cupid;
Bowing, vowing, tearing, swearing,
Lots of horrid lies, declaring
All the love they do *not* feel
For the objects of their zeal.
Of the Poet Milton, I
Prize this observation,
"Sentiment is all my eye,
Bosh and botheration!"

TO MY VALENTINE.

T IS Valentine's morn, love, which sweet little birds
Are by Cupid declared to devote to their wooing,
Addressing their mates in soft twittering words,
And transacting a vast deal of billing and cooing.—
Now if I were a bird, dear, I know what I'd do,
I would rise with the lark, and fly straight to your casement,
Where in ornithological language I'd woo,
'Till you answer'd, "I will," and left off with "Amazement;" *
But not being a bird, my fond wishes alone
Can fly to your presence on wings of the wind,
And while coyly my amiable weakness they own,
Must hint everything pretty, everything kind.

That's the right style of business. Come, don't laugh.
For young birds, tho' not old ones, are taken with chaff,

---
* *Vide* end of Marriage Service.

And I'd have you to know, Miss, such chaff as I've
    written,
Is sweet food, wherewith sundry young birds have been
    smitten;
And if you've the bad taste my soft lines to despise,
I shall deem it a proof that you're more *nice* than wise!
Enclosed is a bracelet, but firmly I swear it,
That she who's my Valentine only shall wear it;
So, dear, decide, will you take it, or leave it?
Ah, the bracelet is yours! by that smile I perceive it.

1856.

FOR M. S.

DO not ask thy love,
The tender joy, the deep emotion,
Of loving woman's fond devotion,
I do not seek to prove.
My path on earth is lonely,
And ever must be, only
In memory of days gone by,
When thou didst smile, and weep, and I
Grew, oh! so happy, in each radiant smile;
Or if the while,
A tear upon thy damask cheek lay sleeping,
Then for thy sake I fell in love with weeping;—
In memory of those days of joy and sorrow,
Sad thoughts, and fancies airy,
*Breathe thy first sigh to-morrow,
For me, Mary!*

Saint Valentine's Eve, 1847.

A DAY DREAM.

HERE are bright and happy hours
In this dwelling-place of tears,
Sunny gleams between the showers,
Merry birds and smiling flowers,
  Hopes that conquer fears.

There are many sweets that mingle
In the cup of mortal sadness;
Fairy bells that softly tingle
By woodland way and forest dingle,
  Moving hearts to gladness.

There are fairer, brighter things,
Star-like gem the path of life:
Sympathy that ever brings
Friendship on its dove-like wings;
Faithful love till death that clings
  Peace, the sleep of strife.

GATHERED LEAVES.

Thus I mused one soft spring morn,
While her clear soprano ringing,
The nightingale was sweetly singing
From her seat in the old thorn;
Then methought that at my side
Harshly thus a voice replied—

" Dreamer, as you name each blessing,
With your gaze upon the sky
Wrapp'd in a fool's fantasy,
Tell me which art thou possessing?"

And at these strange words I wonder'd,
But the bird was singing still,
And an echo from the hill
Seemed to ask me why I ponder'd.

Then I answer'd musingly,
" Love, the urchin, ever roving
To and fro, still passes by,
Glancing with a roguish eye,
Leaving me unloved, unloving.

" Better so, for love," I said,
" Flashes like a meteor gleam;

GATHERED LEAVES.

And realities but seem
Harsher by the light it shed.

"I have many a loving friend;
With their pleasant voices near me,
And their sympathy to cheer me,
I will wear life to its end.

"And when death has had his will
Sparkling eyes for me will weep,
Loyal hearts a corner keep,
For our friendship's memory still."

GATHERED LEAVES.

EPITAPH.

HERE lies Belinda! sad her early doom!
Should perjured Cymon e'er approach her
tomb,

These simple lines her tragic fate impart—
"A check'd flirtation settled on her heart!"

LINES FOR MUSIC.

READ not the dark to-morrow,
    Never weep,
Waking is full of sorrow,
    Prithee sleep!
Sleep shall bright visions yield thee,
    Angel forms
With their soft wings shall shield thee
    From Life's storms:
With their calm eyes behold thee,
    On thee smile,
In their fond arms enfold thee,
    For a while.
Then, when thine eyes unclosing
    Thou shalt wake,
Ev'n from that soft refreshing
    Comfort take.
Nor in life's darkest hour
    Vainly sigh,
Prayer hath mighty power,
    God is nigh!

GATHERED LEAVES.

TO ———.

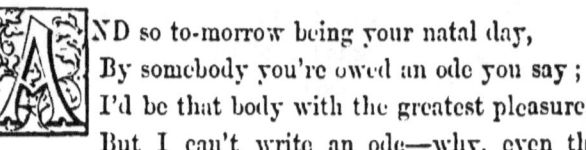ND so to-morrow being your natal day,
By somebody you're owed an ode you say;
I'd be that body with the greatest pleasure,
But I can't write an ode—why, even the measure
"My spirit knows not:" then, another thing,
I lack the where-with-all to say or sing—
I can't find matter. Now were I your lover
A thousand tender nothings I'd discover—
A sonnet to your eyebrow—I don't doubt you
Have such a feature as that same about you;
But for my life I don't believe upon it
I could compose that slow affair, a sonnet.
Let's try—"Hail, lovely eyebrow!"—no,
That's what I classically term "no go."
Eyebrows won't pay; none but a lover amorous
Could on so very mild a theme grow clamorous.
And woe betide *your* lover; I've my doubts
That you're a little flirt, or thereabouts;
One who for years has sacrificed, *sans* scruples,
Whole generations of enamour'd pupils.

Were I their tutor thus I'd wisely preach
'Gainst woman's wiles a remedy to teach:
" Fond youths beware—her dangerous presence fly,
To sigh for Polly were bad policy;
Whate'er your principles, Low Church or High,
Avoid that error, Mary-olatry."

And yet I know not, while I write a feeling
Akin to what they call compunction's stealing
Across me—men ere now have sought the noose
Of marriage with a much less fair excuse.

GATHERED LEAVES

Perhaps you're not a flirt, or if you are
There are worse things than flirting extant, far.
The unconscious coquetry a pretty woman
Displays by nature only proves her human—
Just to be sweetly arch, and mildly spiteful,
But makes her, *entre nous*, the more delightful.
In short, dear Mary, let's for once be friends,
And as my rudeness asks some slight amends
I'll wish you on your birthday wishes three
Health, happiness, and last not least shall be
That *summum bonum* termed "*un bon parti;*"
But when you've got them, and enjoy them rarely
Don't quite forget your loving friend Frank Fairlegh.

LINES WRITTEN TO MISS AUGUSTA SHORT.

O long for Short, and yet to long in vain,
Is little short of bitter longing pain;
Too short a time I've known thee, or too long,
I'm too short-sighted to tell right from wrong;

Nor can I note old Father Time's variety,
Enchanted in such short and sweet society.

GATHERED LEAVES.

But when each short angelic visit's o'er
The long and lazy hours progress no more.
Happy the man who gives thy father's daughter
A longer name (it cannot well be shorter :
He need not envy the exalted station
Of Albert, husband to the British nation,
Around whose princely brow all honours cluster,
For though the Queen's August, yet you're Augusta!

THE LOVER'S REBUKE TO HIS HEART.

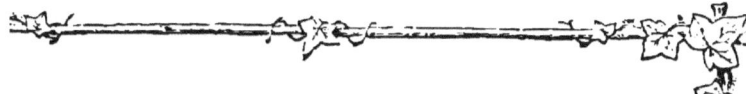HY dost thou start,
Thou foolish, flutt'ring heart?
She is not near;
Or if that she were here,
Why need her gentle presence thus alarm thee?
She would not harm thee.
When through the woodland ways
My lady strays,
All timid things that fly
Man's company
Come forth to meet her;
With songs the wild birds greet her.
Then, foolish, flutt'ring heart, it is my will
That thou lie still."

THE HEART'S REPLY.

ASTER," the heart replied,
    " When 'gainst thy side,
My prison-house, I strike with wild emotion,
  'Tis not with coward fear
    I tremble here,
But an excess of anxious love's devotion.
Thou say'st the presence of thy peerless dame
    Maketh all wild things tame;
    Then grant me liberty
      To her to fly.
  Dear master, we must part,
  For thou hast lost thy heart;
Yet grieve not, nor with sorrow hang thy head,
    For if I once may rest
      Upon her breast,
I'll gain for thee her loving heart instead."

THE PRAYER OF THE WEARY HEART.

OH give me rest! the toil of life,
The petty cares, the petty strife,
The hourly crosses that apart
   From deeper griefs consume my heart,
And leave a desolation there
Akin to, if 'tis not, despair.
                These call for rest.

Oh give me rest! for youth is gone;
And middle-age comes darkly on,
Experience has been hardly bought,
Ambition palls, and Fame is nought;
With chary measure Faith is given,
And Hope is dead, and Love's in heaven.
                I pant for rest.

Oh give me rest! the curse for sin
Was life-long toil; but death came in
A blessing in disguise to free
God's felons from their misery;

GATHERED LEAVES.

The prison-term of life being o'er,
The weary heart will ache no more,
            For death is rest.

Yes, death is rest; beyond the grave
Dim forms their mystic pinions wave;
Repentance yet may pardon move,
For angels fell, and God is love.
We know in part, in part we see,
" Ye heavy-laden come to Me
            And I will give you rest."

REPLY.

I.

OWARD heart, no more repining,
　　Cease to weep,
Greatness dwelleth in resigning,
　　Steadfast keep.
Heed not though the years pass by thee;
Each bright thing that they deny thee
Might have proved a curse to try thee,
　　Dark and deep.

II.

Woman's love in youth's bright morning,
　　Silly heart;
Woman's love may change to scorning,
　　May depart.
Couldst thou gain affection's treasure,
'Tis a fond and fleeting pleasure,
Cruel death hath ta'en its measure,
　　With his dart.

GATHERED LEAVES.

III.

Dost thou pant for man's approving?
    'Tis the sand;
With each idle zephyr moving
    O'er life's strand.
Write thy name! let crowds adorn it!
Ere the waves of time pass o'er it,
Some new idol shall before it
    Proudly stand.

IV.

Noble heart, be true, be earnest
    Watch and wait,
Good for evil thou returnest,
    That is great!
Brave heart, all true honour lies
In a life-long sacrifice,
Stars shine clear above the skies,
    Conquer fate!

1851.

A SONG.

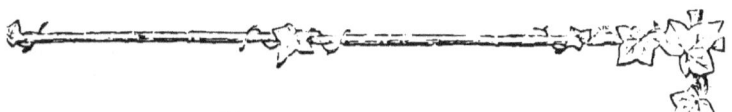EARY, weary life,
　　Wilt thou never cease?
　　　Aching, aching heart,
　　Canst thou ne'er find peace?
　Ever dost thou leave me
False hope and unkind?
　Still wilt thou deceive me
Cruel faith and blind?

　Sunshine of my spirit,
Thou too soon hast fled—
　Wearily I wander,
Youth and love are dead;
　Life unloved, unloving,
Darker than the grave,
　Death from grief removing,
Death alone can save.

GATHERED LEAVES.

Sleep, thy drowsy pinions
O'er my eyelids move,
Still my throbbing pulses,
Let me dream of love;
Give me back the seeming
Of the hopes that were;
Thus perchance may dreaming
Calm awhile despair.

LOVED BEST.

OVED best!" As one with parch'd and
burning lips,
That part to rave in fever's wild unrest,

Quaffs the cool cup, and eager sips and sips,
So eager drink some ears the words, "Loved best."

GATHERED LEAVES.

As sighs the captive in his dungeon pent,
On the stone couch his weary limbs have prest,
Till life, and hope, and energy are spent,
So sigh some aching hearts the words, "Loved best."

As breathes the south wind o'er some happy vale,
Kissing the wild flowers to their dreamless rest,
And ling'ring o'er their beauties sweet and frail,
So breathe some favour'd lips the words, "Loved best."

Loved best, this earth is heaven, unloved 'tis hell!
Death finds a refuge, and the grave gives rest:
Pray for that soul when sounds its passing knell,
Has pined a lifetime for the words, "Loved best."

AT HOME.

I.

HY we meet, why part again,
God alone can tell,
All the pleasure, all the pain,
In His counsels dwell.

II.

Friend, this life is drear and lone,
And we wander to and fro,
As the swallows come and go,
Seeking rest, and finding none.

Friend, this life is very strange,
Whence we came, or where we go,
We may guess, but cannot know,
All seems chance and change.

Friend, there is a life to come,
All is order'd for the best,
Aching hearts shall there find rest,
May *we* meet *at Home!*

GATHERED LEAVES.

TO L. K. Y.

(WITH A PRESCRIPTION.)

I PASS'D by night through the deserted streets;
Calm stars gazed down from out the tranquil sky;
Pensive policemen linger'd on their beats,
With aspect of serene authority;

The busy hum of men no longer greets
The listening ear; for all in slumber lie.
Then, as the moonbeams cool'd my throbbing brow,
I thought of thee, and of my plighted vow.

GATHERED LEAVES.

There are who basely promise, and forget,
Or, perjured, to the ear their promise keep,
But lie to the intent—a shallow set
The first, the last, unprincipled but deep.
Thy friend was not of these; he would not let
Falsehood profane his lips; so ere asleep
He fell, he tied his handkerchief in what
Witlings might term a don't-forget-me knot.

He roused at daybreak—that is, he turn'd out
Just before nine o'clock; and like the rose,
Sprinkled with heavy wet (I don't mean stout),
He sought to blow, but could not; for his nose
Met with a Gordian knot, entwined about
In many a tortuous fold. I don't propose
To tell you what he said, but, if he spoke
A naughty word, it must have been in joke.

Reminded of his promise, then he sent
For a prescription by one Dr. Stone,
Wherein are hieroglyphics which are meant
To tell us that in all mild cases one,
In more severe ones two pills, must be spent
Upon the patient; when six hours have flown,
To be repeated; and he hopes, *sans* scoffing,
Alike they'll save you from your cough and coffin!

A SERENADE.

BREATHE cool on my forehead, soft breeze
of the night,
My brow that is throbbing,

My brow that is burning,
My cheeks fever flushing, my lips quivering white;

Creep close to my bosom, and nestle thee there.
My heart, wildly beating, will give thee glad greeting,
    To still its despair;
Will give thee glad greeting, and welcome thy meeting,
    Bright spirit of air,
Although on thy pinions cold death thou shouldst bear.

I love, and she loves not; she dreams while I weep.
    My eyes, never closing,
    Obtain no reposing,
But under her window their sad vigil keep.
I love, and she loves not; the tale is so old,
The tale is so dreary, the ages are weary
    Of hearing it told;
And yet repetition, with doleful addition,
    Shows others enroll'd
In this army of martyrs to proud hearts and cold.

A REMONSTRANCE.

WHY dost thou bless me, dear one,
　　With thy love so bright and warm?
For I am a dark and a lonely thing,
A wild bird drooping with broken wing,

An oak by lightning shiver'd and scathed,
A beetling rock by the wild waves laved,

GATHERED LEAVES.

Cold and stern and lonely;
Pierced by the arrow, rent by the storm.
    Why shouldst thou glad me only
    With thy love so tender and warm?

    Why should thy smiles, sweet sunshine,
    Rest on my saddened brow?
The wounded eagle pines alone;
Flowers blossom not on the cold grey stone;
And the ivy that clings to the shattered oak
Clings but to fall 'neath the woodman's stroke.
    Weary thought and carking care,
Deep have they traced their furrows e'en now.
    Why should thy smiles, sweet sunshine,
    Rest on my throbbing brow?

GATHERED LEAVES.

"ALONE."

TILL o'er the trackless sea of life
  My bark toils wearily alone;
  Alone I stem the wild waves' strife,
  And hear the sad wind's plaintive moan.

Far from each shore of calm content,
From sunny islands of delight,
Alone my cheerless course is bent,
No sun by day, no star by night.

Alone I watch the drifting cloud,
And list the sea-bird's boding cry;
Alone, like ghost in circling shroud,
I view the pale foam gliding by.

Alone, dark thoughts assail my breast,
Wild wishes, sad regrets, which tear
The heartstrings with a fierce unrest
That mocks the calmness of despair.

Regrets! alas, regrets are vain;
Tumultuous longings all pass by;
If wish be left me, 'tis again
To rest on one loved heart—and die.

GATHERED LEAVES.

LILY FLOWER.

RUSTING hearts are oft betray'd,
   Shady bower, treach'rous bower,
Fickle youth and silly maid,
      Heedless Lily Flower.

He was comely and tall to view,
Keen of eye, but of heart untrue;
That, alas! she little knew,
      Simple Lily Flower.

Eglantine and heartsease grew
   Round the shady bower.
Spring was young, and he seem'd true,
      Happy Lily Flower.

Summer blossoms soon have past;
Bending 'neath the autumn blast,
Dost thou guess the truth at last,
      Drooping Lily Flower?

GATHERED LEAVES.

Hangs the cold, relentless snow
On the leafless bower.
Man's false love brings woman's woe,
        Fading Lily Flower.

No loving hand was there to save,
Heav'n has ta'en the life it gave.
Lay her in her early grave,
        Weep for Lily Flower.

GATHERED LEAVES.

SAINT PÈRE.

LOVE thee not, and yet relief
Gladdens my soul, when thou art near,
And all dear things seem still more dear,
And sorrow loses half its grief.

I do not love thee, yet 'tis sweet
To tell thee all my inner life,
And how I strive or fail in strife,
And sit disciple at thy feet.

Thou art so strong where I am weak;
And when perchance my narrower mind
Meets cruel deed with word unkind,
Thou teachest gentler phrase to speak.

I do not love thee, yet thy smile
Sheds such sweet sunshine o'er my heart,
I can but sit and weep apart,
When shadows cloud thy brow awhile.

I love thee not with human love,
When passion with its fierce unrest
Gladdens or rends the throbbing breast,
And weary earth seems heaven above.

As dying saint, we part adore
Part mourn, and still would gladly give
A thousand lives to bid him live,
So love I thee, nor less nor more.

January, 1862.

A CHARACTER.

ERY good eyes which are train'd to express
Things inexpressible, what I can't guess;
Mouth rather wide, but a rare one for
    chattering
Smart observations and compliments flattering;

Hair black by candle-light, seen in the day,
Entre nous, it is slightly "chenhilled" with grey.

Something red for a headdress the dark locks enclosing,
Quite original, neat, picturesque, and imposing.
Gown, the simple white muslin of sweet seventeen,
Most outrageously bustled with stiff crinoline,
Short sleeves and long body, made, dear me, Oh fye!
Most excessively low where it ought to be high.
Impertinent shoulders, by way of variety,
Protruded, denuded, defying propriety,
As a last forlorn hope of some marrying "spec"
She now strives, like a race-horse, to *win by a neck*.
Then she sings tragic songs up to concert pitch taught,
With expression all borrow'd, and feeling all bought,
She sighs forth the woes of some desolate maid
With a heart smash'd to bits, and affections betray'd,
And she flirts most tremendously fast when she can,
Which is every time she addresses a man.
"Is that you, Mr. D? Lor! I am so surprised!
Where's my poor little rosebud you told me you
    prized?
Lost! I'll never forgive you, you promised to save it.
Is that a forget-me-not? Yes, you may have it.
Don't lose that! Must you go? Well, I hope I shall
    see
You to-morrow. Ah! How do you do, Mr. B."
Thus reversing the proverb, she thinks it's the thing
To possess, flirting double, two *beaux* to her string.

GATHERED LEAVES.

She's a capital memory, talks of the stage
In the year '28, when Sontag was the rage,
Which unwise retrospection quite makes one think
    (ought I
To conceal the idea?) that she's not far from forty.

HOPE ON, HOPE EVER!

THERE are who deem it best,
    To make of love a jest,
A pleasant sport on Valentine's fair
    morning;
    But to such triflers I
    Would gravely thus reply,
Take heed lest careless loving call forth scorning.

    Then to my lady fair
    Will I my love declare,
Ever in warmest and in briefest measure;
    As men the casket mould,
    Of brightest, purest gold,
Which shall contain their rarest, costliest treasure.

    Dear one, if you and I,
    Loving, could live and die,
This darksome earth would be as fair as heaven;
    But lonely tears and woe
    Are our sad lot below,
Until repented sins shall be forgiven.

GATHERED LEAVES.

Over each beauteous thing
Yet the dark shadows cling,
Shades that descend from sinning and from sorrow;
But when the night is past,
Dawn shall appear at last,
Bright with the glory of the long to-morrow.

ODE.

EEMING the rhymer's art was mine,
Thou badst me write a valentine,
And gavest me as fair a theme
As e'er inspired poet's dream;
Saying, my guerdon rare should be
A bright and sunny smile from thee;
And I that dear reward to win
Would fain at once the task begin.

Despite the raven voice of fate,
Which tells of twelve long months to wait,
E'er time again on circling wing,
Saint Valentine's fair morn shall bring—
Astute Minerva! goddess high!
Deign to assist thy votary;
Come to my aid, and bring with thee
Thine handmaid, ingenuity;
And help me with some cunning wile
To cheat old Time, and win "the smile."
Thanks, for the bright idea,
'Tis said her natal day draws near.

GATHERED LEAVES.

Might not a birthday ode obtain
The recompense I pant to gain?
'Tis a fair scheme, and boldly I
Resolve at once the chance to try;
For still the proverb true we trace,
"Faint heart ne'er won fair lady's grace."
Wait a bit, not so fast, 'tis a horrible plague;
 But I'm free to confess
 What perhaps you won't guess,
 (For in one who writes verses
 No ignorance worse is),
My ideas of an ode are excessively vague:
 'Tis true I've read loads
 Of Horace's odes.
There's the first, which no doubt at the time had a
 great run,
In which he "soft sawders" Mæcenas his patron,
 And tells him he springs
 From a race of old kings.
 Then there's "Olim jam satis,"
 Which nought very great is;
And another to Lydia,
Where he calls her "candidior
Nives," which epithet doubtless you know
Refers to her skin, and means "whiter than
 snow."

GATHERED LEAVES.

But these odes are all Latin, and Latin won't do
    To send to a lady, unless "she's a blue;"
Which, thank goodness, you're not, for there's nothing
    more shocking
Than that pedant in petticoats term'd a blue stocking.
One who stuffs down your throat without any apology
A succession of horrors all ending in "ology."
        Or, by way of variety,
        Favours society.
With her private opinion respecting broad gauges,
The potato disease, or the low rate of wages:
        No, depend on it, blue
        Is a hose that won't do.
The best test that young ladies can choose for their
    hose,
And their minds, and their ribbons, is "couleur de
    rose."
    But stay, I'm forgetting my ode all this time,
    It behoves me to alter the style of my rhyme,
    And rejecting the comic, attempt the sublime.

    Hail to the happy hour that gave thee birth!
        When first on earth
    Those beaming eyes so eloquently bright
        Beheld the light!

GATHERED LEAVES

Gaily spring flowers blossom'd on that day,
Young gladsome birds the budding sprays among
    Burst forth in festal song,
    And deemed it May.
Hail to the day that marks thy womanhood!
    All wishes good
Attend thee, and preserve thee as thou art,
    True of heart;
And innocent and happy, for thy years
Have yet been few; and still perchance to thee
    Seems it, earth cannot be
    A vale of tears.
Long may it be, e'er sorrow's ebon wing
    It's shadows fling
O'er that fair face, or quench that sunny smile
    In tears the while.
But if some tears must fall, may it be given,
When still the troubled spirit finds relief
    For every grief
    From Heaven!

    There, I'm sure that's enough
    Of such serious stuff,
    I can't write any more,
    'Tis no end of a bore.

GATHERED LEAVES.

I suppose that's an ode, if it's not I can't tell
What it is; but no doubt it will do just as well.
Thus, I think, I may reckon my labours are done,
And lay claim to "the smile" as a prize fairly won.
So, fair lady, you'd better get ready for granting one,
And, Carina, take care it's a very *enchanting one!*
But should you prove false, or refuse to bestow it,
You may (mark my words, for I wish you to know it),
Find some other to flirt with, and get a new poet!

LEBE WOHL!

EBE wohl, ach! lebe wohl!
Words of grief too often spoken:
Dear sister of my inmost soul,
With tearful eyes and hearts half broken!
Yet 'twas not thus we parted, no!
One pressure of the heart, one sigh,
One glance from half averted eye,
Was all the sign that spoke our woe.
Yet ever as some parting knell
Rings on mine ear that word farewell.

Lebe wohl, ach! lebe wohl!
Weary leagues of distance sever,
Angry waves between us roll,
Parting now may prove for ever.
But should it be so, still to me,
When half my soul is from me reft,
One source of happiness is left,
Of bygone hours the memory—
Even farewell no gloom can cast
O'er bright reflections of the past.

GATHERED LEAVES.

Lebe wohl, ach! lebe wohl!
Say, dost thou ever think upon
The happy moments that we stole
(Too brief, perchance for ever gone),
When midst the gay and careless throng,
Apart we spake of holy things,
High thoughts and bright imaginings,
Flowers strewn the path of life along.
Farewell was then no word of sorrow,
We parted, but to meet to-morrow.

Lebe wohl, ach! lebe wohl!
For months, for years, or till at last
For us the funeral bell may toll,
To say another soul has pass'd.
Then if our faith be not in vain,
Nor vain th' inspiring hope that Heaven
To prayer and penitence is given,
My sister, we may meet again
Where love eternal rests alone,
And farewell is a word unknown

GATHERED LEAVES.

IN VAIN?

"HAVE lived and loved in vain!"
True, as far as this life goes.—
Have I lived and loved in vain?
God, who knows the future, knows.

Is there then a life to come?
Shall again the "dry bones" live?
One alone can call us *home*,
God the giver, let Him give.

LINES WRITTEN FOR THE BAZAAR

FOR THE

Windsor New Free and Industrial Schools.

ING a song of sixpence, a pocket full of rye!"
We quote a nursery lyric, and we're going to tell you why.
We are about to sing a song, and sing for money, too;
But "rye" will not *our* pockets fill, nor yet will "sixpence do."
We want good Queen Victoria's head, with its bright golden hair,
Emboss'd upon a *golden* coin, as fits a gem so rare:
Nor can the brain of wit or sage a better change suggest,
For Sovereign such as England boasts, than that which we request.
In letters six we'll briefly state what may our object be—
To teach poor children A B C, we want your £ s. d.
Small brats who through the streets run wild, and lisp the tongue vehicular,
Term'd slang, we'll send to infant schools to shout out "Perpendicular,"

As they point their little fingers to the rafters overhead,
And to murmur "Horizontal" when they lie them
    down in bed.
Then older boys shall know the joys of adding and
    subtracting,
And "rule of three" less puzzling be when business
    is transacting.
Or if we get our "Buttons" through a course of
    "vulgar *fractions*,"
Our crockery may suffer less from his untaught exac-
    tions.
Then at our hands the softer sex shall due attention
    claim,
Each little child shall curtsey if we only breathe her
    name;
The elder girls being taught to wash and iron, bake and
    boil,
Stiff starch we'll wear, and praise hard fare, first pro-
    ducts of their toil.
To sew her "Edwin's" buttons on we'll teach each
    "Angelina,"
And rustic swains will thus be kept much better fed
    and cleaner.
Therefore, good friends, the more you give to help our
    good intentions,
The better we can carry out our notable inventions;

GATHERED LEAVES.

But even if with all your aid we can't reform society,
We should on the old crab-stock, man, engraft a new variety.
If we should teach some simple child the narrow path to tread,
Boldly to brave the fight of life, and rest its weary head
Where true rest only can be found, you not in vain have given
Your gold or silver mite towards the treasury of Heaven.

FRANK FAIRLEGH.

THE END.

LONDON:
PRINTED BY JAMES S. VIRTUE,
CITY ROAD.

BY FRANK E. SMEDLEY.

I.

Post 8vo., 2s. 6d. boards, or 3s. 6d. in cloth, gilt back,

FRANK FAIRLEGH;
OR, SCENES FROM THE LIFE OF A PRIVATE PUPIL.

* A Library Edition, with 30 Illustrations by George Cruikshank, 8vo., 16s. cloth.

II.

Post 8vo., 3s. boards, or 4s. in cloth, gilt backs,

LEWIS ARUNDEL;
OR, THE RAILROAD OF LIFE.

* A Library Edition, with 42 Illustrations by H. K. Browne ("Phiz"), 8vo., 22s. cloth.

III.

Post 8vo., 2s. 6d. boards, or 3s. 6d. in cloth, gilt back,

HARRY COVERDALE'S COURTSHIP, AND ALL THAT CAME OF IT.

* A Library Edition, with 30 Illustrations by H. K. Browne ("Phiz"), 8vo., 16s. cloth.

IV.

Third Edition, Fcap. 8vo., illustrated by "Phiz," 1s. 6d. boards, or 2s. 6d. in cloth, gilt back and side,

THE FORTUNES OF THE COLVILLE FAMILY;
OR, A CLOUD AND ITS SILVER LINING.

LONDON: VIRTUE BROTHERS AND CO., 1, AMEN CORNER.

BY S. M.

I.

Crown 8vo., 7s. 6d.,
TWICE LOST.

II.

Two Vols., Fcap., 12s.,
LINNET'S TRIAL.

III.

Fcap. 8vo., 2s. 6d.,
NINA: A Tale of the Twilight.

IV.

Fcap. 8vo., two vols. in one, 2s. 6d.,
THE STORY OF A FAMILY.

V.

Second Edition, Fcap., 2s. 6d.
THE USE OF SUNSHINE.
A CHRISTMAS NARRATIVE.

EDITED BY FRANK E. SMEDLEY.
Second Edition, Fcap., 2s. boards, or 2s. 6d. cloth,
SEVEN TALES BY SEVEN AUTHORS.

The Mysteries of Redgrave Court .	By F. E. Smedley.
Norfolk and Hereford	„ G. P. R. James.
The Will	„ Miss Pardoe.
King Veric	„ M. F. Tupper.
The Last in the Lease	„ Mrs. S. C. Hall.
A Very Woman	„ Miss M. B. Smedley.
"The Trust"	„ Mrs. Burbury.

LONDON: VIRTUE BROTHERS AND CO., 1, AMEN CORNER.

JANUARY, 1865.

GENERAL CATALOGUE

OF WORKS PUBLISHED BY

VIRTUE BROTHERS & CO.,

1, AMEN CORNER, LONDON.

NEW BOOKS.

SHOWELL'S HOUSEKEEPER'S ACCOUNT BOOK, exhibiting every description of expense likely to occur in a family, with Tables showing at one view the amount expended Weekly, Quarterly, and the Whole Year, in every department, and the total amount of cash received and expended in one year. To which is added the Cook's Almanack and Diary of Good Living. 4to., interleaved with Blotting Paper, 2s.

THE ART-JOURNAL, Monthly, price 2s. 6d.; and in Yearly Volumes, cloth, 31s. 6d. each. Volume for 1864, cloth gilt, £1 11s. 6d.

GATHERED LEAVES. A Collection of the Poetical Works of the late FRANK E. SMEDLEY, Author of "Frank Fairlegh." With a Memorial Preface by EDMUND YATES, a Portrait, and numerous humorous designs. Printed on superior paper, with Borders. Imperial 16mo. imitation half-morocco, gilt edges, 8s. 6d. [*Just Published.*

ORIGINAL POEMS FOR INFANT MINDS. In 1 Vol., Illustrated by H. ANELAY, with various designs by J. & G. NICHOLLS. Fcap. cloth gilt, 5s. [*Just Published.*

THE HISTORY OF CARICATURE AND GROTESQUE IN Literature and Art. By THOMAS WRIGHT, M.A., F.S.A. With Illustrations by F. W. FAIRHOLT. [*Just Ready.*

GOING TO THE DOGS; or, the Adventures of Frank. Showing how he was brought up to follow neither Trade nor Profession, and what his very genteel bringing up brought him to. By C. G. ROWE, Author of "What put my Pipe out; or, Incidents in the Life of a Clergyman," &c. Fcap. cloth, 3s. 6d.

CAMPION COURT. A Tale of the Days of the Ejectment, Two Hundred Years Ago. By EMMA JANE WORBOISE, Author of "Lottie Lonsdale," "The Lillingstones," &c. Second Edition. Fcap. cloth, 5s.

THE LIFE OF THOMAS ARNOLD, D.D. By EMMA JANE WORBOISE. Second Edition. Fcap. cloth, 3s. 6d. [*In the Press.*

FAMOUS GIRLS WHO HAVE BECOME ILLUSTRIOUS WOMEN; forming Models of Imitation to the Young Ladies of England. By JOHN M. DARTON. Fcap. cloth gilt, 3s. 6d.; with Illustrations, 5s.

STEPS AND STAGES ON THE ROAD TO GLORY. By the Author of "Our Heavenly Home," "Truths for the Day of Life and the Hour of Death," &c. Fcap. cloth, 5s.

a

CATALOGUE OF WORKS

THE RE-ISSUE OF "PUNCH." Containing a large number of Illustrations by the late John Leech. In 20 volumes, 1840-1861. Originally published at £10 5s. 6d., now offered for 7 guineas in cloth, gilt edges; or £8 in cloth gilt, gilt edges; or imitation half-morocco gilt edges, £8.

OUTLINES OF MODERN FARMING. By R. SCOTT BURN. 2 vols. Illustrated, 12mo. cloth, 14s. *Or separately—*
Part 1. Soils, Manures, and Crops. 2s.
Part 2. Farming Economy, Historical and Practical. 3s.
Part 3. Cattle, Sheep, and Hors s. 2s. 6d.
Part 4. Dairy, Pigs, and Poultry. 2s.
Part 5. Utilisation of Town Sewage, Irrigation, and Reclamation of Waste Land. 2s. 6d.

A HANDY BOOK ON THE LAW OF FRIENDLY, INDUSTRIAL AND PROVIDENT, BUILDING, AND LOAN SOCIETIES. With Copious Notes. By NATHANIEL WHITE, Esq. 12mo., 1s.

PRACTICAL HINTS FOR INVESTING MONEY: with an Explanation of the Mode of Transacting Business on the Stock Exchange. By FRANCIS PLAYFORD, Sworn Broker. Third Edition, revised and corrected. 12mo., 1s.

A TREATISE ON LOGIC. By S. H. EMMENS, Esq. 12mo., 1s.

THE STEPPING STONE TO ARITHMETIC. By A. ARMAN. 1s. KEY, 1s.

ELEMENTARY TREATISE ON SAILS AND SAILMAKING; with Draughting, and the Centre of Effort of the Sails. Also, Weights and Sizes of Ropes; Masting, Rigging, and Sails of Steam Vessels, &c. By ROBERT KIPPING, N.A., Sailmaker, Quayside, Newcastle, Author of "Treatise on Mast Making and Rigging of Ships," &c. Seventh Edition, enlarged. Illustrated. 2s. 6d.

ART-JOURNAL (THE), Monthly, price 2s. 6d.; and in Yearly Volumes, cloth, 31s. 6d. each. No. I. of a New Series was commenced 1 January, 1862.

———————— VERNON GALLERY. Series 1849 to 1854.

———————— ROYAL GALLERY. Series 1855 to 1861.

———————— TURNER GALLERY. Series 1862-1863.

———————— ILLUSTRATED CATALOGUE OF THE GREAT INDUSTRIAL EXHIBITION OF 1851, containing upwards of 1,400 Engravings on Wood, and Frontispiece on Steel. 4to. cl., gilt edges, 21s.

———————————————————— INTERNATIONAL EXHIBITION OF 1862. Illustrated with nearly 1,500 Engravings on Wood, and 12 on Steel. Royal 4to. cloth gilt, gilt edges, 21s.

ACKWORTH VOCABULARY, or English Spelling-Book; with the Meaning attached to each Word. Compiled for the use of Ackworth School. 18mo. cloth, 1s. 6d.

ADAMS' (W. H. D.) SCENES FROM THE DRAMA OF EUROPEAN HISTORY. P st 8vo. cloth, 6s.

AIKEN (DR.) and BARBAULD (MRS.), EVENINGS AT HOME. New Edition. With Illustrations by HARVEY. Fcap. cloth, 3s. 6d.

PUBLISHED BY VIRTUE BROTHERS AND CO.

ALFRED DUDLEY. 16mo. cloth gilt, 2s. 6d.

ANALYSIS AND SUMMARY OF OLD TESTAMENT HIS-
TORY AND THE LAWS OF MOSES, with a connection between the Old
and New Testaments, an Introductory Outline of the Geography, Political
History, &c. By J. T. WHEELER, F.R.G.S. Ninth Edition, post 8vo.
cloth, red edges, 5s. 6d.

——————————— NEW TESTAMENT HIS-
TORY; including, 1. The Four Gospels harmonised into one continuous
Narrative. 2. The Acts of the Apostles, and continuous History of St.
Paul. 3. An Analysis of the Epistles and Book of Revelation. 4. An
Introductory Outline of the Geography, Critical History, Authenticity,
Credibility, and Inspiration of the New Testament. The whole Illustrated
by copious Historical, Geographical, and Antiquarian Notes, Chronological
Tables, &c. Seventh Edition, revised. Post 8vo. cloth, red edges, 5s. 6d.

——————————— A POPULAR ABRIDG-
MENT OF OLD AND NEW TESTAMENT HISTORY, for Schools,
Families, and General Reading. Explained by Historical and Geographical
Illustrations, and numerous Map Diagrams. 2 Vols. 18mo. cloth, 2s. each.

——————————— WHEELER'S HISTO-
RICAL GEOGRAPHY OF THE OLD AND NEW TESTAMENTS.
Illustrated with Five coloured Maps, and large View of Jerusalem, with a
Plan of the Ancient City. Folio, cloth, 7s. 6d.

ASBURY (F.), THE PIONEER BISHOP, LIFE OF, by
STRICKLAND. Post 8vo. cloth, 2s.

BARBAULD'S (Mrs.) LECONS POUR DES ENFANTS, depuis
l'âge de Deux Ans jusqu'à Cinq. Avec une Interprétation Anglaise.
New Edition. 18mo. cloth, 2s.

——————— HYMNES EN PROSE, pour les Enfans, traduites
de l'Anglaise par M. Clemence. 18mo. limp cloth, 1s.

BARCLAY'S UNIVERSAL ENGLISH DICTIONARY. New
Edition. By B. B. WOODWARD. Numerous Engravings and Maps. 4to. cl., 32s.

BARNES' NOTES ON THE NEW TESTAMENT, Critical and
Explanatory. With Introduction by the Rev. H. STEBBING. Steel Engravings. 2 Vols., 4to. cloth, £2 8s.

BARTLETT'S (W. H.) FOOTSTEPS OF OUR LORD AND
HIS APOSTLES. Royal 8vo., cloth gilt, 10s. 6d.

——————— FORTY DAYS IN THE DESERT. Royal 8vo.,
cloth gilt, 10s. 6d.

——————— GLEANINGS ON THE OVERLAND ROUTE.
Royal 8vo. cloth gilt, 10s. 6d.

——————— JERUSALEM REVISITED. Royal 8vo. cloth
gilt, 10s. 6d.

——————— NILE-BOAT. Royal 8vo. cloth gilt, 10s. 6d.

——————— PICTURES FROM SICILY. Royal 8vo. cloth
gilt, 10s. 6d.

——————— PILGRIM FATHERS. Royal 8vo. cl. gilt, 10s. 6d.

CATALOGUE OF WORKS

BARTLETT'S SCRIPTURE SITES AND SCENES. 12mo.
cloth, gilt edges, 4s.

———— WALKS ABOUT JERUSALEM. Royal 8vo.
cloth gilt, 10s. 6d.

BASKET OF FLOWERS; or, Piety and Truth Triumphant. A
Tale for the Young. 32mo. cloth, gilt edges, 1s.

BEATTIE'S (W.) CASTLES AND ABBEYS OF ENGLAND.
Illustrated by BARTLETT. 2 Vols. royal 8vo. cloth, each 25s.

BELLENGER'S ONE HUNDRED CHOICE FABLES, in
French, imitated from LA FONTAINE. With DICTIONARY of Words and
Idiomatic Phrases, Grammatically Explained. New Edition, revised by
C. J. DELILLE. 12mo. cloth, ts. 6d.

BELLEW'S (REV. J. C. M.) SHAKESPERE'S HOME AT NEW
PLACE, Stratford-upon-Avon. Illustrated. Post 8vo. cloth, gilt top, 12s.

BIBLE, BROWN'S SELF INTERPRETING. With Plates.
Royal 4to. cloth, £2 2s.

———— With MATTHEW HENRY's Commentary. Edited and
Abridged by Rev. E. BLOOMFIELD. Illustrated. 2 Vols. 4to. cloth, £2 15s.

———— With Commentary by Rev. T. SCOTT. Unabridged. 3 Vols.
royal 4to. cloth, £4 4s.

———— THE DOUAY (Roman Catholic) TRANSLATION.
Edited by F. C. HUSENBETH. 52 Plates. 2 Vols. 4to. cloth, £3.

BLYTHE HOUSE. By R. F. H. Crown 8vo. cloth, 6s.

BOOK OF BRITISH SONG. With Pianoforte Accompaniments.
By HOGARTH. 2 Vols. folio, cloth, each 21s.

BRENAN'S (JUSTIN) COMPOSITION AND PUNCTUATION,
familiarly explained for those who have neglected the Study of Grammar.
Twelfth Edition, 12mo., limp cloth, 1s.

BROWN'S (J.) DICTIONARY OF THE BIBLE. 2 Vols.
8vo. cloth, 22s.

BROWN'S (R.) TREATISE ON DOMESTIC ARCHITEC-
TURE. 4to. cloth, £2 2s.

BROWN'S (T.) MANUAL OF MODERN FARRIERY. 8vo.
cloth, 13s. 6d.

———————————— With Instructions in Hunting, Fishing,
and Field Sports. 8vo. cloth, 20s.

BUNYAN'S PILGRIM'S PROGRESS, Pictorial Edition. Illustrated by 97 fine Engravings on Wood. Also many Engravings on Steel,
with a Portrait and Facsimile of John Bunyan's Will. Royal 8vo. cl., 18s.

———— HOLY WAR. Uniform with the above. Numerous
Illustrations. Royal 8vo. cloth, 12s.

———— ENTIRE WORKS. Edited, with Original Intro-
ductions, Notes, and Memoir, by the Rev. H. STEBBING. Illustrations on
Steel and Wood. 4 Vols. large 8vo., £2 12s.

BURN'S (ROBERT SCOTT) OUTLINES OF MODERN FARMING.
Vol. I.—Soils, Manures, and Crops. 12mo. limp cloth. Illustrated. 2s.

——————————————— Vol. II. Farming Economy, Historical and Practical. 12mo. limp cloth. Illustrated. 3s.

——————————————— Vol. III. Stock — Cattle, Sheep, and Horses. 12mo. limp cloth. Illustrated. 2s. 6d.

——————————————— Vol. IV. Management of the Dairy—Pigs—Poultry. 12mo. limp cloth. Illustrated. 2s.

——————————————— Vol. V. Utilisation of Town Sewage—Irrigation—Reclamation of Waste Land. 12mo. limp cloth. Illustrated. 2s. 6d.

——————————————— The above 5 vols. bound in 2, cloth boards, 14s.

BURNET'S (JOHN) LANDSCAPE PAINTING IN OIL-COLOURS EXPLAINED. With Examples. Re-edited by H. MURRAY. 4to. cloth, 12s.

——————— PRACTICAL HINTS ON PORTRAIT-PAINTING, illustrated with Examples. Re-edited by H. MURRAY. 4to. cloth, 12s.

BURNS' COMPLETE WORKS. With Notes and Life, by ALLAN CUNNINGHAM; and a copious Glossary. Illustrated by 33 Engravings (or 61 Engravings), and Portrait. Royal 8vo. cloth, gilt edges, 18s.; or with Supplement, £1 4s.

BUTLER'S (ALBAN) LIVES OF THE SAINTS. Edited by HUSENBETH. 2 Vols. royal 8vo. cloth, £2 5s.

BYRON'S POETICAL WORKS (Pictorial Edition). Fine Engravings. R yal 8vo. cloth, £1 3s.

CAMPBELL'S (COLONEL WALTER) OLD FOREST RANGER; or, Wild Sports of India on the Neilgherry Hills, the Jungles, and the Plains. New Edition, with Illustrations on Steel. Small 8vo. cloth, 8s.

——————— (ISABELLA), MEMOIR OF; or, Peace in Believing. 18mo. cloth, 2s. 6d.

CAMPION COURT. A Tale of the Days of the Ejectment Two Hundred Years Ago. By E. J WORBOISE, Author of "Lottie Lonsdale," "The Lillingstones," &c. Second Edition. Fcap. cloth, 5s.

CANADIAN CRUSOES; a Tale of the Rice Lake Plains. By Mrs. TRAILL, authoress of "The Backwoods of Canada," &c. Edited by AGNES STRICKLAND. With numerous Illustrations by HARVEY. Fcap. cloth, 2s. 6d.

CARLILE (REV. J., D.D.),—MANUAL OF THE ANATOMY AND PHYSIOLOGY OF THE HUMAN MIND. Crown 8vo. cloth, 4s.

CARTWRIGHT (BACKWOODS PREACHER), AUTOBIOGRAPHY OF. The Birth, Fortunes, and General Experiences of the oldest American Methodist Travelling Preacher. Edited by W. P. STRICKLAND. Post 8vo. cloth, 2s.

CHRISTIE'S CONSTRUCTIVE ETYMOLOGICAL SPELLING-BOOK. New Edition, 12mo. cloth, 1s. 6d.

CITY SCENES; or, a Peep into London. With many Plates. 16mo. cloth, 1s. 6d.

COLA MONTI; or, the Story of a Genius. A Tale for Boys. By the Author of "How to win Love." With Four Illustrations by FRANKLIN. Fcap. cloth, 2s. 6d.

COOPER'S SURGICAL DICTIONARY. New Edition. Vol. I. 8vo. cloth, 25s.

CULPEPPER'S BRITISH HERBAL AND FAMILY PHYSICIAN, to which is added a Dispensatory. 8vo. cloth, 16s.

By the REV. J. CUMMING, D.D., F.R.S.E.

APOCALYPTIC SKETCHES. New Edition. 3 Vols. fcap. cloth, 18s.

——————— Original Edition. 3 Vols. cloth, 3s. 6d. each.

BAPTISMAL FONT. Fcap. 1s.; cloth, gilt edges, 2s.

CHRIST OUR PASSOVER. Fcap. cloth, 1s. 6d.

CHURCH BEFORE THE FLOOD. Fcap. cloth, 3s. 6d.

COMFORTER. Fcap. cloth, 1s. 6d.

COMMUNION TABLE. Fcap. sewed, 1s. 6d.; or cloth, 3s.

CONSOLATIONS. Fcap. cloth, 5s.

DAILY FAMILY DEVOTION. 4to. cloth, with Plates, 21s.

DAILY LIFE. Fcap. cloth, 3s. 6d.

FINGER OF GOD. Fcap. cloth, 1s. 6d.

FORESHADOWS; or, Lectures on our Lord's Miracles. Fcap. cloth, 3s. 6d.

——————— Parables. Fcap. cloth, 3s. 6d.

HAMMERSMITH PROTESTANT DISCUSSION, between the Rev. JOHN CUMMING, D.D., and DANIEL FRENCH, Esq. Tenth Thousand. Post 8vo. cloth, 6s.

INFANT SALVATION. Fcap. 1s.; gilt edges, 2s.

IS CHRISTIANITY FROM GOD? Fcap. cloth, 3s.

JOSEPH THE LAST OF THE PATRIARCHS. Fcap. cloth, 6s.

LECTURES AT EXETER HALL; or, a Challenge to Cardinal Wiseman. Fcap. cloth, 2s. 6d.

LECTURES ON THE SEVEN CHURCHES. Fcap. cloth, 3s. 6d.

LECTURES TO YOUNG MEN. Crown 8vo. cloth, 6s.

MESSAGE FROM GOD. Fcap. 1s.; gilt edges, 2s.

BY THE REV. J. CUMMING, D.D., F.R.S.E.—*continued*.

OUR FATHER. Fcap. cloth, gilt edges, 3s.

PSALTER OF THE BLESSED VIRGIN. Written by ST. BONAVENTURE. 12mo. cloth, 2s.

PSALMS AND PARAPHRASES, according to the Version of the Church of Scotland, with supplement Hymns and Doxologies. 12mo. cloth, 3s. 6d.; roan, 5s.; morocco, 6s. 6d.

RUTH; A CHAPTER IN PROVIDENCE. Fcap. cloth, 3s. 6d.

SABBATH EVENING READINGS ON THE NEW TESTAMENT. 13 Vols. fcap. cloth, £3 9s. 6d.

Or, separately—

MATTHEW. 5s.
MARK. 3s.
LUKE. 6s.
JOHN. 6s.
ACTS. 7s.
ROMANS. 4s. 6d.
CORINTHIANS. 5s.
GALATIANS, &c. 6s.
COLOSSIANS, &c. 4s. 6d.
TIMOTHY, &c. 4s.
HEBREWS. 5s.
JAMES, &c. 6s.
REVELATIONS. 7s. 6d.

SCRIPTURE READINGS ON THE OLD TESTAMENT. SAMUEL. Fcap. cloth, 5s. DANIEL. Fcap. cloth, 3s. KINGS. Fcap. cloth, 4s. 6d.

SALVATION. Sermon before the Queen. Sewed, 6d.

SIGNS OF THE TIMES. Fcap. cloth, 3s. 6d.

TENT AND THE ALTAR. Cheap Edition. Fcap. cloth, 3s. 6d.

THINGS HARD TO BE UNDERSTOOD. Fcap. cloth, 7s.

THY WORD IS TRUTH. Fcap. cloth, 5s.

WAR AND ITS ISSUES. Fcap. cloth, 1s. 6d.

WELLINGTON. Fcap. cloth, 1s. 6d.

DALTON (WM.), THE TIGER PRINCE; or, Adventures in the Wilds of Abyssinia. With 8 Illustrations. Post 8vo. cloth, 5s.

DARTON'S (J. M.) FAMOUS GIRLS WHO HAVE BECOME ILLUSTRIOUS WOMEN; forming Models of Imitation to the Young Ladies of England. Fcap. cloth gilt, 3s. 6d. With Illustrations, 5s.

DARTON (MARGARET E.), THE EARTH AND ITS INHABITANTS. With Frontispiece. Second Edition, crown 8vo. cloth, 5s.

DAVIS'S (REV. N.) EVENINGS IN MY TENT; or, Wanderings in the African Sahara. With Illustrations. 2 Vols., post 8vo. cloth, 24s.

DECOY (THE); or, An Agreeable Method of Teaching Children the Elementary Parts of English Grammar. 18mo., 6d.

DESLYON'S FRENCH DIALOGUES, to enable all Persons at once to practise Conversing in French; with FAMILIAR LETTERS in FRENCH and ENGLISH. 12mo. cloth, 2s. 6d.

——————— TUTOR; or, Exposition of the best French Grammarians, with Exercises and Questions on every Rule, for Examination and Repetition. 12mo. cloth, 4s.

DICKSEE'S (J. R.) SCHOOL PERSPECTIVE. A Progressive Course of Instruction in Linear Perspective. 8vo. cloth, 5s.

DOCTOR'S LITTLE DAUGHTER (THE). The Story of a Child's Life amidst the Woods and Hills. By ELIZA METEYARD. With numerous Illustrations by HARVEY. Fcap. cloth, gilt edges, 5s.

DRESSER'S (C.) RUDIMENTS OF BOTANY, Structural and Physiological. Being an Introduction to the Study of the Vegetable Kingdom. 8vo. cloth, 15s.

——————— UNITY IN VARIETY, as Deduced from the Vegetable Kingdom. 8vo. cloth, 10s. 6d.

DYING COMMAND OF CHRIST (THE); or, the Duty of Believers to Celebrate Weekly the Sacrament of the Lord's Supper. By the Author of "God is Love," "Our Heavenly Home," &c. Fcap. cl., 2s. 6d.

EDGEWORTH'S (MARIA) MORAL TALES. Fcap. cloth, 3s. 6d.

——————— POPULAR TALES. Fcap. cloth, 3s. 6d.

——————— EARLY LESSONS. Fcap. cloth, 3s. 6d.

——————— 4 Vols. 18mo. cloth, 10s.

——————— PARENT'S ASSISTANT. Fcap. cloth, 3s. 6d.

——————— HARRY AND LUCY. 3 Vols. fcap. cl. 10s. 6d.

——————— From "Early Lessons." 18mo. cloth, 2s. 6d.

——————— ROSAMUND. From "Early Lessons." 18mo. cloth, 2s. 6d.

——————— FRANK. From "Early Lessons." 18mo. cloth, 2s. 6d.

FAIRHOLT'S (F. W.) DICTIONARY OF TERMS IN ART. Numerous Woodcuts. Post 8vo. cloth, 10s. 6d.

FLEETWOOD'S (REV. J., D.D.) LIFE OF CHRIST. With an Essay by Rev. H. STEBBING. With 58 Steel Engravings. 4to., cloth, £1 9s.

FLETCHER'S (REV. ALEXANDER, D.D.) GUIDE TO FAMILY DEVOTION. Portrait, and 24 Engravings. 4to., cloth, gilt edges, £1 6s.

——————— NEW EDITION, with Portrait and 25 Plates. Royal 4to., cloth gilt edges, £1 8s.

——————— CLOSET DEVOTIONAL EXERCISES FOR THE YOUNG, from Ten Years Old and upwards. Post 8vo. cloth, 5s.

——————— SCRIPTURE HISTORY. For the Improvement of Youth. With 241 Engravings on Steel. 2 Vols. 18mo., cloth gilt, 18s.

PUBLISHED BY VIRTUE BROTHERS AND CO. 9

FLETCHER'S SCRIPTURE NATURAL HISTORY. 256 Engravings on Steel. 2 Vols., 16mo. cloth, 20s.

———— ASSEMBLY'S CATECHISM. Divided into 52 Lessons. 12mo. sewed, 8d.

———— SCRIPTURE TEXTS. 12mo. sewed, 6d.

———— BOOK OF PROVERBS. 12mo. sewed, 6d.

———— HYMNS. 24mo. roan, 3s.

FRANK FAIRLEGH; or, Scenes from the Life of a Private Pupil. By F. E. SMEDLEY, Esq. Cheap Edition, boards, 2s. 6d.; cloth, 3s. 6d., or with 30 Illustrations by GEORGE CRUIKSHANK, 8vo. cloth, 16s.

FRANKLIN'S (BENJAMIN) WORKS AND LIFE. 8vo. cloth, 8s.

FULLER'S (ANDREW) WORKS AND LIFE. Edited by his Son. Royal 8vo. cloth, 24s.

GEMS OF EUROPEAN ART. Edited by Mrs. S. C. HALL. 96 Steel Plates. 2 Vols., folio cloth gilt, £5.

GIBBON'S DECLINE AND FALL OF THE ROMAN EMPIRE. With Memoir, and Additional Notes, from the French of M. GUIZOT. Numerous Engravings and Maps. 2 Vols. super-royal 8vo. cloth, £1 16s.

GILES'S (JAMES) ENGLISH PARSING. Improved Edition. 12mo. cloth, 2s.

GILFILLAN'S THE MARTYRS, HEROES, AND BARDS OF THE SCOTTISH COVENANT. Fcap. cloth, 2s. 6d.

GOING TO THE DOGS; or, the Adventures of Frank. Showing how he was brought up to follow neither Trade nor Profession, and what his very genteel bringing up brought him to. By C. G. ROWE, Author of "What put my Pipe out; or, Incidents in the Life of a Clergyman," &c. Fcap. cloth, 3s. 6d.

HACK'S (MARIA) STORIES OF ANIMALS. Adapted for Children from Three to Ten Years of Age. 16mo. cloth, 1s. 6d.

———— WINTER EVENINGS; or, Tales of Travellers. With 8 Illustrations by GILBERT and HARVEY. New Edition. Fcap. cloth, 3s. 6d.

HALL'S (MR. AND MRS. S. C.), IRELAND; its Scenery, Character, &c. 48 Steel Plates and 500 Woodcuts. 3 Vols. royal 8vo. cl., £3 3s.

———— WEEK AT KILLARNEY. Illustrated with Woodcuts. Royal 8vo. cloth, 8s.

———— HANDBOOK FOR IRELAND. Post 8vo. cloth, 8s.

———— BOOK OF SOUTH WALES; THE WYE, AND THE COAST. Numerous Engravings. Fcap. 4to. cloth gilt, 15s.

———— BOOK OF THE THAMES, FROM ITS RISE TO ITS FALL. With numerous Engravings. Fcap. 4to. cloth gilt, 16s.

HAPPY TRANSFORMATION ; or, History of a London Apprentice. With Preface by Rev. J. A. James. 18mo. cloth, 6d.

HARRY COVERDALE'S COURTSHIP, AND WHAT CAME OF IT. By Frank E. Smedley. Post 8vo. bds., 2s. 6d.; cloth, 3s. 6d. or, with Illustrations by Hablot K. Browne, 8vo. cloth, 16s.

HENDRY'S HISTORY OF GREECE. In Easy Lessons. For Children of Six to Ten Years of Age. With Illustrations. 18mo. cl., 2s.

────── HISTORY OF ROME. In Easy Lessons. For Children of Six to Ten Years of Age. With Illustrations. 18mo. cloth, 2s.

HENRY'S (Matthew) COMMENTARY ON THE HOLY BIBLE. Abridged by the Rev. E. Blomfield. With 50 Engravings. 2 Vols. 4to. cloth, £2 15s.

HISTORY OF ENGLAND DURING THE REIGN OF GEORGE III. By John George Phillimore, Q.C. Vol. I. 8vo. cl., 18s.

HOOPER'S (Mrs.) RECOLLECTIONS OF MRS. ANDERSON'S SCHOOL. New Edition, with 4 Illustrations. Fcap. cloth, 3s. 6d.

HOPKINS' ORTHOGRAPHICAL EXERCISES. New Edition. 18mo. cloth, 1s. 6d.

HOW TO WIN LOVE; or, Rhoda's Lesson. A Story Book for the Young. By the Author of "Michael the Miner," "Cola Monti," &c. With Illustrations on Steel. New Edition, 16mo. cloth, gilt edges, 2s. 6d.

HOWITT'S (William) A BOY'S ADVENTURES IN THE WILDS OF AUSTRALIA. Cuts by Harvey. Fcap. cloth gilt, 4s.; Cheap Edition, without Illustrations, 2s.

HUME AND SMOLLETT'S HISTORY OF ENGLAND. With a Continuation to the Year 1860, by Dr. E. H. Nolan. 108 Plates and Maps, engraved on Steel. 3 Vols. imperial 8vo., cloth gilt, £3 3s.

────── With Continuation by Farr to the Year 1846. 3 Vols., royal 8vo. cloth, £2 12s. 6d.

JERDAN'S (W.) AUTOBIOGRAPHY. 4 Vols. Post 8vo. cl., 21s.

JOBSON'S (F. J.) AMERICA AND AMERICAN METHODISM. Post 8vo. cloth, 7s. 6d.

JOSEPHUS (The Works of). With Essay by Rev. H. Stebbing. 80 Woodcuts, and 46 Steel Engravings. Royal 8vo., cloth gilt, £1 5s.

LAURIE (James),—TABLES OF SIMPLE INTEREST FOR EVERY DAY IN THE YEAR, at 5, 4½, 4, 3½, 3, and 2½ per cent. per annum, from £1 to £100, &c. Twenty-seventh Edition, 800 pp. 8vo. cloth, strongly bound, £1 1s.; or in calf, £1 6s.

────── TABLES OF SIMPLE INTEREST, at 5, 6, 7, 8, 9, and 9½ per cent. per annum, from 1 day to 100 days. Eighth Edition, 8vo. cloth, 7s.

LAURIE'S UNIVERSAL EXCHANGE TABLES, showing the value of the coins of every country interchanged with each other, at all rates of exchange, from One Coin to One Million Coins. 8vo. cloth, £1.

―――― TABLES OF EXCHANGE between Paris, Bordeaux, Marseilles, Havre, Lyons, Brussels, Ghent, Bruges, Antwerp, Genoa, and London. 8vo., bound in calf, £1.

―――― MADEIRA EXCHANGE TABLES. Being Portuguese and British Money reduced into each other. 8vo. cloth, 6s.

―――― MANUAL OF FOREIGN EXCHANGES. Being British Coins reduced into Twenty-eight of the Principal Countries of the World, &c.; also from One to One Million Coins of these countries in decimals of the £, with French and Turkish exchanges. 4th Edition, 32mo. 9d.

―――― EXPOSITOR OF FOREIGN EXCHANGES. Being British Coins reduced into Twenty-four of the Principal Countries of the World; in parallel columns, &c. &c. On a sheet royal, folded in a book, 3s.

―――― FOREIGN AND BRITISH SHARE TABLES, from 1s. 3d. to £100 per share, in British and Decimal Moneys, &c. 12mo. cl., 12s.

―――― GOLDEN READY RECKONER, calculated in British Money and Dollars, showing the value from One Ounce to One Hundred Thousand Ounces Gold, Platina, Silver, Goods and Merchandise of every description, Shares in Public Companies, &c. &c. 12mo. cloth, 12s.

―――― DECIMAL COINAGE. A Practical Analysis of the Comparative Merits of £1 and 10d. as the Ruling Integer of a Decimal Currency for the United Kingdom. 8vo. sewed, 2s. 6d.

LAWSON (A.),—MODERN FARRIER. 8vo. cloth, 13s. 6d.

LE PAGE'S FRENCH COURSE.

"The sale of many thousands, and the almost universal adoption of these clever little books by M. LE PAGE, sufficiently prove the public approbation of his plan of teaching French, which is in accordance with the natural operation of a child learning its native language."

FRENCH SCHOOL. Part I. L'ECHO DE PARIS. Being a Selection of Familiar Phrases which a person would hear daily if living in France. Price 3s. 6d. cloth.

KEY TO DITTO; or, Finishing Exercises in French Conversation. Price 1s. sewed.

FRENCH SCHOOL. Part II. THE GIFT OF FLUENCY IN FRENCH CONVERSATION. With Notes. Price 2s. 6d. cloth.

KEY TO DITTO: PETIT CAUSEUR; or, First Chatterings in French. Price 1s. 6d. sewed.

FRENCH SCHOOL. Part III. THE LAST STEP TO FRENCH. With the Versification. Price 2s. 6d. cloth.

PETIT LECTEUR DES COLLEGES; or, the French Reader for Beginners and Elder Classes. A Sequel to "L'Echo de Paris. 12mo. Price 3s. 6d. cloth.

CATALOGUE OF WORKS

LE PAGE'S FRENCH COURSE.—*continued.*

FRENCH MASTER FOR BEGINNERS; or, Easy Lessons in French. Price 2s. 6d. cloth.

JUVENILE TREASURY OF FRENCH CONVERSATION. With the English before the French. Price 3s. cloth.

FRENCH PROMPTER. A Handbook for Travellers on the Continent and Students at Home. Price 4s. cloth.

READY GUIDE TO FRENCH COMPOSITION. French Grammar by Examples, giving Models as Leading-strings throughout Accidence and Syntax. Price 3s. 6d. cloth.

ETRENNES AUX DAMES ANGLAISES. Being a Key to French Pronunciation in all its niceties. Price 6d. sewed.

PETIT MUSÉE DE LITTÉRATURE FRANÇAISE, with Chronological and Critical Notices of the Eminent Writers of France, from the Fourteenth Century to the Nineteenth. Prose, 4s. 6d.; Poetry, 4s. 6d.

LEWIS ARUNDEL; or, the Railroad of Life. By F. E. SMEDLEY, Esq., Author of "Frank Fairlegh." Cheap Edition, 3s. boards; 4s. cloth; or, with Illustrations by H. K. BROWNE (PHIZ), 8vo. cloth, 22s.

LINNET'S TRIAL. A Tale by S. M., Author of "Twice Lost," &c. 2 Vols. fcap. cloth, 12s.

LUTHER, KNOX, THE INQUISITION, NEW ENGLAND. From the "Teacher's Offering." 18mo. cloth, 1s.

M'HENRY'S SPANISH COURSE.

A NEW AND IMPROVED GRAMMAR. Containing the Elements of the Language and the Rules of Etymology and Syntax Exemplified; with Notes and Appendix, consisting of Dialogues, Select Poetry, Commercial Correspondence, &c. New Edition, revised. 12mo. bound, 6s.

EXERCISES ON THE ETYMOLOGY, SYNTAX, IDIOMS, &c., of the SPANISH LANGUAGE. Fifth Edition, 12mo. bound, 3s.

KEY TO THE EXERCISES. 12mo. bound, 4s.

SYNONYMES OF THE SPANISH LANGUAGE EXPLAINED. 12mo. 4s.; and 8vo. 6s.

MACKAY'S (CHAS.) STUDIES FROM THE ANTIQUE, AND SKETCHES FROM NATURE. Fcap. cloth, 3s. 6d.

MANKIND IN MANY AGES. An Outline of Universal History. By Mr. T. L. VON ORDEKOP. Crown 8vo. cloth, 7s. 6d.

MANUAL OF HERALDRY, being a concise Description of the several Terms used, and containing a Dictionary of every Designation in the science. Illustrated by 400 Engravings on Wood. New Edition, fcap. cloth, 3s.

By the Author of "MARY POWELL."

CALIPH HAROUN ALRASCHID (The). Post 8vo. cloth, 2s. 6d.

THE OLD CHELSEA BUN-HOUSE. Cheap Edition, fcap. cloth, 2s. 6d.

MAIDEN AND MARRIED LIFE OF MARY POWELL, Third Edition, with Portrait. Post 8vo. cloth, red edges, 7s. 6d.

CHERRY AND VIOLET. Post 8vo. cloth antique, 3s. 6d.

CHRONICLES OF MERRY ENGLAND. Fcap. 8vo., 3s. 6d.

CLAUDE THE COLPORTEUR. Post 8vo. cloth, 3s. 6d.

COTTAGE HISTORY OF ENGLAND. 12mo. cloth, 2s. 6d.

DAY OF SMALL THINGS (The). Post 8vo. cloth, 7s. 6d.

DEBORAH'S DIARY. Cheap Edition, fcap. cloth, 2s.

———————————— Post 8vo. cloth, 6s.

EDWARD OSBORNE. Cheap Edition, fcap. cloth, 2s. 6d.

ETHELFLED. Post 8vo. cloth antique, 6s.

FAMILY PICTURES. Post 8vo. cloth, 7s. 6d.

GOOD OLD TIMES (The). Post 8vo. cloth, 7s. 6d.

HELEN AND OLGA. Post 8vo., 3s. 6d.

THE HILL SIDE. Fcap. cloth, 1s. 6d.

JACK AND THE TANNER. Post 8vo., 9d.

MORE'S HOUSEHOLD. Cheap Edition, 2s. 6d.

POPLAR HOUSE ACADEMY. Post 8vo. cloth, 7s. 6d.

———————————— 2 Vols. fcap. cloth, 7s. 6d.

PROVOCATIONS OF MADAME PALISSY. Post 8vo. cloth, 3s. 6d.

QUEENE PHILIPPA'S GOLDEN BOOKE. Post 8vo. 3s. 6d.

NOBLE PURPOSE NOBLY WON. Post 8vo. cloth, 7s. 6d.
———————————— 2 Vols. fcap. cloth, 7s. 6d.

SABBATH AT HOME. Post 8vo. cloth, 3s. 6d.

SOME ACCOUNT OF MRS. CLARINDA SINGLEHART. Post 8vo. cloth, 7s. 6d.

TASSO AND LEONORA. Post 8vo. cloth, 3s. 6d.

MEMORABLE EVENTS IN THE LIFE OF A LONDON PHYSICIAN. Demy 8vo. cloth, 7s. 6d.

MIALL'S (EDWARD) BASES OF BELIEF. Crown 8vo. cl., 3s. 6d.

——— CHRISTIAN POLITICS. Crown 8vo. cloth, 3s. 6d.

MILL IN THE VALLEY; a Tale of German Rural Life. By the Author of "Moravian Life." Fcap. cloth, 6s.

MORAVIAN LIFE IN THE BLACK FOREST. Edited by the Author of "Mary Powell." 12mo. cloth, 6s.

MONOD (A.),—WOMAN: HER MISSION AND HER LIFE. From the French by Rev. W. G. BARRETT. Third Edition, 18mo. cl., 1s. 6d.

——————— SAINT PAUL. Five Discourses. Translated from the French by Rev. W. G. BARRETT. 18mo. cloth, 1s. 6d.

MONTAGU'S (LADY M. W.) LETTERS FROM THE LEVANT. Fcap. cloth, 5s.

MOUBRAY'S TREATISE ON DOMESTIC AND ORNAMENTAL POULTRY. By L. A. MEALL; the Diseases of Poultry, by Dr. HORNER. Coloured Illustrations. Fcap. cloth, 3s. 6d.

MY OLD PUPILS. By the Author of "My Schoolboy Days." With Four Illustrations on Wood. 16mo. cloth, gilt edges, 2s. 6d.

NAOMI; or, the Last Days of Jerusalem. By Mrs. J. B. WEBB. With Illustrations by GILBERT, BARTLETT, &c. New Edition, revised and corrected by the Author. Fcap. cl., 7s. 6d.; or in 2nd morocco gilt, 10s. 6d.

NATIONAL GALLERY. Comprising about 150 Engravings from the "Vernon Collection." 3 Vols. royal 4to. cloth, £8 8s.

NICHOLSON'S CARPENTER'S GUIDE; being a Complete Book of Lines for Carpenters, Joiners, Cabinet-Makers, and Workmen in general. Improved Edition. Edited by JOHN HAY. 4to. cloth, £1 11s. 6d.

——— ——— (PETER) PRACTICAL TREATISE ON MENSURATION. A sequel to the "Carpenter's Guide." 4to. cloth, 18s.

NINA; a Tale. By S. M. Fcap. cloth, 2s. 6d.

NOLAN'S (E. H.) HISTORY OF THE BRITISH EMPIRE IN INDIA AND THE EAST. Illustrated. 2 Vols. royal 8vo. cl., £2 5s.

——————— HISTORY OF THE WAR AGAINST RUSSIA. Illustrated. 2 Vols. royal 8vo. cloth, £2 5s.

NURSERY RHYMES. By the Authors of "Original Poems." 18mo. cloth, 1s. 6d.

——————————————— Illustrated. 16mo. cloth, 2s. 6d.

ORACLES FROM THE BRITISH POETS. By JAMES SMITH. Third Edition, fcap. cloth, gilt edges, price 2s. 6d.

ORIGINAL POEMS FOR INFANT MINDS. Illustrated by H. ANELAY, and engraved by J. and G. NICHOLLS. Fcap. cloth gilt, 5s. A Cheap Edition, 2 Vols., 18mo. cloth, 1s. 6d. each.

PUBLISHED BY VIRTUE BROTHERS AND CO. 15

By the Author of "OUR HEAVENLY HOME."

COMFORTER (THE); or, the Holy Spirit in His Glorious Person and Gracious Work. Fourth Edition. Fcap. cloth, 5s.; gilt edges, 5s. 6d.

DYING COMMAND OF CHRIST; or, the Duty of Believers to Celebrate Weekly the Lord's Supper. Fcap. cloth, 2s. 6d.

GRACE AND GLORY; or, the Believer's Bliss in Both Worlds. Fcap. cloth, 5s., gilt edges, 5s. 6d.

GOD IS LOVE; or, Glimpses of the Father's Infinite Affection for His People. Seventh Edition. Fcap. cloth, 5s.; gilt edges, 5s. 6d.

GOD'S UNSPEAKABLE GIFT; or, Views of the Person and Work of Jesus Christ. Third Edition. Fcap. cloth, 5s.; gilt edges, 5s. 6d.

GLEAMS OF GLORY FROM THE CELESTIAL WORLD. 32mo. cloth, 1s.

OUR HEAVENLY HOME; or, Glimpses of the Glory and Bliss of the Better World. Seventh Edition. Fcap. cloth, 5s.; gilt edges, 5s. 6d.

SOURCES OF JOY IN SEASONS OF SORROW. 32mo. cloth, 1s.

STEPS AND STAGES ON THE ROAD TO GLORY. Fcap. cloth, 5s.

THE GLORIOUS GOSPEL OF CHRIST; considered in its Relations to the Present Life. Second Edition. Fcap. cloth, 5s.

THE FOES OF OUR FAITH, AND HOW TO DEFEAT THEM. Fcap. cloth, 5s.

TRUTHS FOR THE DAY OF LIFE AND THE HOUR OF DEATH. Third Edition. Fcap. cloth, 5s.

PARKINSON'S (R.) PROTESTANT CATECHISM. 18mo. sewed, 6d.

PATTIE DURANT; a Tale of 1662. By CYCLA, Author of "Passing Clouds," &c. Fcap. cloth, 2s. 6d.

PAYNE'S (JOSEPH) SELECT POETRY FOR CHILDREN; with brief Explanatory Notes, arranged for the use of Schools and Families. Fourteenth Edition. 18mo. cloth, 2s. 6d.; with gilt edges, 3s.

———— STUDIES IN ENGLISH POETRY; with short Biographical sketches, and Notes Explanatory and Critical, intended as a Text-Book for the higher Classes in Schools. Fifth Edition, enlarged. Crown 8vo. cloth, red edges, 5s.

PEOPLE'S MUSIC BOOK, with Accompaniment for Organ and Pianoforte. By E. TAYLOR and J. TURLE. 3 Vols., royal 8vo. cloth, 36s.; or separately, as Psalm Tunes, Secular Music, and Sacred Music, 12s. each.

PHILLIMORE (JOHN GEORGE),—HISTORY OF ENGLAND DURING THE REIGN OF GEORGE THE THIRD. Vol. I. 8vo. cloth, 18s.

———— REPLY TO THE MISREPRESENTATIONS OF THE EDINBURGH REVIEW, October, 1863. 8vo. sewed, 2s.

PICTORIAL SPELLING-BOOK; or, Lessons on Facts and Objects. With 130 Illustrations. New Edition. 12mo. cloth, 1s. 6d.

PLEASANT PASTIME; or, Drawing-room Dramas for Private Representation by the Young. With Cuts. 16mo. cloth, gilt edges, 2s. 6d.

POOLE'S (MATTHEW) DIALOGUES BETWEEN A POPISH PRIEST AND AN ENGLISH PROTESTANT. By Rev. JOHN CUMMING, D.D. 18mo. cloth, 1s. 6d.

PRINCE OF THE HOUSE OF DAVID; or, Three Years in the Holy City. With Illustrations. Fcap. cloth, 3s. 6d.

REMBRANDT AND HIS WORKS. Illustrated with Examples, by J. BURNET. Re-edited by H. MURRAY. 4to. cloth, 12s.

RHYMES FOR THE NURSERY. By the Authors of "Original Poems." 18mo. cloth, 1s. 6d.

——————————————————— Illustrated Edition, in large type. With 16 Designs by GILBERT. 16mo. cloth, 2s. 6d.

RIPPON'S (DR.) SELECTION OF HYMNS FROM THE BEST AUTHORS, including a great number of Originals, intended as an Appendix to Dr. Watts's Psalms and Hymns. New Editions.

Nonpareil 32mo.	*Long Primer* 24mo.	*Large Type.*
s. d.	s. d.	s. d.
Roan . . . 1 6	Roan . . . 2 6	Sheep . . . 5 0
——, gilt edges 2 0	——, gilt edges 3 0	Roan, gilt edges 6 0
Morocco . . . 5 0	Morocco . . . 6 0	Morocco . . . 9 0

ROBINSON CRUSOE. With Illustrations. 18mo. cloth, 2s.

ROWE'S (C. G.) GOING TO THE DOGS; or, the Adventures of Frank. Showing how he was brought up to follow neither Trade nor Profession, and what his very genteel bringing up brought him to. Fcap. cloth, 3s. 6d. [*Just Published.*

ROLLIN'S ANCIENT HISTORY. 2 Vols. 8vo. cloth, 21s.

ROWBOTHAM'S (J., F.R.S.A.) DERIVATIVE SPELLING-BOOK. 12mo. cloth, 1s. 6d.

——————————————————— GUIDE TO THE FRENCH LANGUAGE AND CONVERSATION; consisting of Modern French Dialogues, with the Pronunciation. New Edition, by DE LA VOYE. 1emo. bound, 2s. 6d.

ROYAL GEMS FROM THE GALLERIES OF EUROPE; with Descriptions by S. C. HALL. 2 Vols. Elephant folio cloth, £5.

RURAL SCENES; or, a Peep into the Country. A New and Revised Edition, with 88 Cuts. 18mo. cloth, 2s.

RUTTER'S (Roman Catholic) LIFE OF CHRIST. Edited by F. C. HUSENBETH. Plates. 4to. cloth, 2s

RYALL'S PORTRAITS OF EMINENT CONSERVATIVES. 72 Plates. 2 Vols., foli , cloth, £6.

SANDFORD AND MERTON. With Cuts. 18mo. cloth, 2s.

SCOFFERN'S (Dr.) CHEMISTRY NO MYSTERY. Illustrated. Fcap. cloth, 2s. 6d.

SCOTLAND (THE PICTORIAL HISTORY OF). Edited by the Rev.
J. TAYLOR, D.D. Illustrated with 79 Engravings on Steel, from Drawings by W. H. BARTLETT, and other Artists. 2 Vols., imperial 8vo., £2 5s.

SCOTT (REV. T.),—HOLY BIBLE, with Readings, an Abridged Commentary, and 28 Engravings. 16mo. roan, embossed, 5s. 6d.; morocco, 7s.; elegant, 7s. 6d.

SCULPTURE (GALLERY OF MODERN). 80 Steel Plates. With Descriptions. Folio, cloth gilt, £3 3s.

SHAKESPERE'S COMPLETE WORKS. With Notes and Introduction by H. STEBBING With Illustrations. Royal 8vo. cloth. 25s.

SHARPE'S NEW TESTAMENT. Translated from GRIESBACH's Text. Fourth Edition. Fcap. cloth, 1s. 6d.

SHELMERDINE'S SELECTION OF THE PSALMS and other Portions of Scripture, arranged and marked for Chanting. Fcap. cloth, 1s.

——————— ONE HUNDRED AND FIFTY CHANTS, Selected from the most famous composers. Crown 8vo. cloth, 2s. 6d.

By FRANK E. SMEDLEY.

FRANK FAIRLEGH. Crown 8vo. boards, 2s. 6d.; cloth, 3s. 6d.; or with 30 Illustrations by GEORGE CRUIKSHANK, 8vo. cloth, 16s.

HARRY COVERDALE'S COURTSHIP. Crown 8vo. boards, 2s. 6d.; cl., 3s. 6d.; or, with Illustrations by H. K. BROWNE, 8vo. cl., 16s.

LEWIS ARUNDEL. Crown 8vo. 3s. boards; cloth, 4s.; or with Illustrations by H. K. BROWNE (PHIZ), 8vo. cloth, 22s.

THE COLVILLE FAMILY. Frontispiece and Vignette Title by PHIZ. Fcap. boards, 1s. 6d.; cloth, 2s. 6d.

SEVEN TALES BY SEVEN AUTHORS. Edited by the Author of "Frank Fairlegh." Fcap. 2s. boards; 2s. 6d. cloth.

SMITH (C. M.), THE LITTLE WORLD OF LONDON. Post 8vo. cloth, 3s. 6d.

——————— THE DEAD LOCK. A Story in Eleven Chapters. Also, TALES OF ADVENTURE. Post 8vo. cloth, 3s. 6d.

SPURGEON (REV. C. H.),—THE SAINT AND HIS SAVIOUR; or, The Progress of the Soul in the Knowledge of Jesus. With Portrait. Fcap. cloth gilt, 6s.

STEPS AND STAGES ON THE ROAD TO GLORY. By the Author of "Our Heavenly Home," &c. Fcap. cloth, 5s.

STORY OF A FAMILY. By S. M. Fcap. cloth, 2s. 6d.

STORY WITHOUT AN END. Translated from the German by SARAH AUSTIN. Illustrated by HARVEY. New Edition. 16mo. cloth, bevelled boards, 2s. 6d.

SWAIN'S (CHARLES, Author of "The Mind," "English Melodies," &c.) ART AND FASHION; with other Sketches, Songs, and Poems. Post 8vo. cloth, 7s. 6d.

TATE'S ELEMENTS OF COMMERCIAL ARITHMETIC. Fifth Edition. 12mo. cloth, 2s. 6d. KEY, 3s. 6d.

TAYLOR'S (JAMES) PICTORIAL HISTORY OF SCOTLAND, from the Roman Invasion to the Close of the Jacobite Rebellion, A.D. 79—1746. 2 Vols. royal 8vo. cloth, £2 5s.

TAYLOR'S (BP.) LIFE OF CHRIST. Edited by PHILIP. 4to. cloth, 10s. 6d.

THOMSON'S (A.) CONSOLATIONS FOR CHRISTIAN MOURNERS. 8vo. cloth, 12s.; 12mo. cloth, 5s.

TOMLINSON'S (CHAS.) EXPERIMENTAL ESSAYS. 1. On the Motions of Camphor on the Surface of Water. 2. On the Motion of Camphor towards the Light. 3. History of the Modern Theory of Dew. With Illustrations. 12mo. limp cloth, 1s.

——————————— CYCLOPÆDIA OF USEFUL ARTS, Mechanical and Chemical, Manufactures, Mining, and Engineering. Illustrated by upwards of 2,500 Engravings on Steel and Wood. 2 Vols. Royal 8vo. cloth, £2 5s.

TRAILL'S (MRS.) LADY MARY AND HER NURSE; or, a Peep into the Canadian Forest. Fcap. cloth, 2s. 6d.

TREASURE-SEEKER'S DAUGHTER. 12mo. bds., 1s.

TREDGOLD ON THE STEAM ENGINE. In Two Sections: 1. MARINE ENGINES. 2. LOCOMOTIVE AND STATIONARY ENGINES. 1000 pages of Text, and upwards of 220 Engravings. Also 160 Woodcuts and Diagrams. 3 Vols. royal 4to. cloth, £4 14s. 6d.

By **MARTIN F. TUPPER, D.C.L., F.R.S.**

CITHARA: a Selection from the Lyrical Writings of M. F. Tupper. Post 8vo. cloth, gilt edges, 5s.

KING ALFRED'S POEMS. Fcap. cloth, 3s.

THE CROCK OF GOLD, THE TWINS, AND HEART. Post 8vo, 2s. 6d. boards; or separately, 1s. 6d. each, cloth.

PROVERBIAL PHILOSOPHY. Translated into French. Portrait. Fcap. cloth, 2s. 6d.

TURNER AND HIS WORKS. Illustrated with Examples from his Pictures, and Remarks by J. BURNET, and Memoir by P. CUNNINGHAM. Re-edited by H. MURRAY. 4to. cloth, 12s.

TWICE LOST. A Novel in One Volume. By the Author of "Story of a Family," "Queen Isabel," &c. Crown 8vo. cloth, 7s. 6d.

TYTLER'S (M. Frazer) TALES OF MANY LANDS. With
Eight Illustrations. New Edition. Fcap. cloth, 6s.

VAUX'S (W. S. W., M.A.) NINEVEH AND PERSEPOLIS;
an Historical Sketch of Ancient Assyria and Persia. Fourth Edition, with
numerous Illustrations. Post 8vo. cloth, 3s. 6d.; or gilt, 5s.

VERNON GALLERY (The). Comprising about 150 Engravings.
4 Vols. folio, cloth, £8 8s.

VIRTUE'S ILLUSTRATED WORKS—Demy 4to., gilt edges.

AMERICAN SCENERY. 120 Plates, after Sketches by
W. H. Bartlett. Descriptions by N. P. Willis, Esq. 2 Vols., £1 15s.

THE BOSPHORUS AND THE DANUBE. The Bosphorus by Miss Pardoe. The Danube by W. Beattie, M.D. Illustrated with 170 Engravings. 4to. 2 Vols., £1 5s. each.

CALEDONIA ILLUSTRATED. 150 Engravings, from
Drawings by W. H. Bartlett and T. Allom, &c. The literary portion
by William Beattie, M.D. 2 Vols., £2 10s.

CANADIAN SCENERY. 2 Vols., £1 15s.

IRELAND (Scenery and Antiquities of). 120 Engravings,
by W. H. Bartlett. Descriptive Text by J. Stirling Coyne, N. P.
Willis, &c. 2 Vols., £1 15s.

PALESTINE (Christian in); or, Scenes of Sacred History.
80 Engravings, from Drawings by W. H. Bartlett. Descriptions by
H. Stebbing. £1 5s.

PIEDMONT AND ITALY, from the Alps to the Tiber.
Illustrated. By Dudley Costello. The artistic department by Harding,
Pyne, Bartlett, Brockedon, &c. 2 Vols., £2 2s.

PORTS AND HARBOURS OF GREAT BRITAIN.
A Series of 144 Views of all the points of interest round the entire Coast.
2 Vols., £2.

SCOTLAND. By W. Beattie. Illustrated in a Series of
Views, by Allom, Bartlett, and M'Culloch. 2 Vols. £2.

SWITZERLAND ILLUSTRATED. By Dr. Beattie, the
Drawings by W. H. Bartlett. 2 Vols., £2.

WALDENSES (The); or, Protestant Valleys of Piedmont,
Dauphiny, &c. By W. Beattie. Illustrated by Bartlett and Brockedon. £1 5s.

WATTS' AND RIPPON'S HYMNS. Bound in One Volume,
32mo. roan, embossed, sprinkled edges, 3s., gilt edges, 3s. 6d.

WATTS' (Dr.) DIVINE AND MORAL SONGS FOR CHILDREN. With Anecdotes and Reflections, by the Rev. Ingram Cobbin, M.A.
Frontispiece and 57 Woodcuts. New Edition, cloth, 1s.; gilt edges, 1s. 6d.

WEBB'S (Mrs. J. B.) NAOMI; or, the Last Days of Jerusalem.
With View, &c. of Jerusalem, and 15 Illustrations by GILBERT and BARTLETT. Fcap. cloth, 7s. 6d.; or in 2nd morocco, gilt, 10s. 6d.

WHEELER'S (J. T., F.R.G.S.) HANDBOOK TO THE COTTON CULTIVATION IN THE MADRAS PRESIDENCY. With Map and Illustrations. Post 8vo. cloth, 7s. 6d.

——————— HISTORICAL GEOGRAPHY OF THE OLD AND NEW TESTAMENTS. Folio cloth, 7s. 6d.

——————— ANALYSIS AND SUMMARY OF OLD TESTAMENT HISTORY AND THE LAWS OF MOSES. Tenth Edition. Post 8vo. cloth, red edges, 5s. 6d.

——————— ANALYSIS AND SUMMARY OF NEW TESTAMENT HISTORY. Sixth Edition. Post 8vo. cloth, red edges, 5s. 6d.

——————— POPULAR ABRIDGMENT OF OLD AND NEW TESTAMENT HISTORY. 2 Vols. 18mo. cloth, 2s. each.

WILKIE GALLERY. A Selection of Engravings from the Paintings of the late Sir DAVID WILKIE, R.A. Cloth gilt, £3 10s.

WILLEMENT (E. E.), A CATECHISM OF FAMILIAR THINGS. New Edition, Fcap. cloth, 2s. 6d.

——————— BIRDS AND ANIMALS. Cuts. 12mo. cloth, 2s.

WOODWARD'S (B. B.) WALES (THE HISTORY OF), From the Earliest Times to its Final Incorporation with England. Illustrated by Views of Remarkable Places, Antiquities, and Scenery. 2 Vols., super-royal 8vo., cloth gilt, £1 5s.

WORBOISE'S (E. J.) CAMPION COURT. A Tale of the Days of the Ejectment Two Hundred Years Ago. Second Edition. Fcap. cl., 5s.

——————— THE LILLINGSTONES OF LILLINGSTONE. Fcap. cloth, 5s.

——————— LOTTIE LONSDALE; or, the Chain and its Links. Second Edition. Fcap. cloth, 5s.

WRIGHT'S (THOMAS, ESQ., M.A., F.S.A.) THE CELT, THE ROMAN, AND THE SAXON. A History of the Early Inhabitants of Britain. Illustrated by the Ancient Remains brought to light by recent research. Numerous Engravings. New Edition. Post 8vo. cloth, 12s.

——————— DOMESTIC MANNERS AND SENTIMENTS IN ENGLAND DURING THE MIDDLE AGES. With numerous Illustrations by F. W. FAIRHOLT, Esq. Fcap. 4to. cloth gilt, price 21s.

YOUNG MAN'S COMPANION. By J. MAVOR, F.S.A. 10 Engravings on Steel. 8vo. cloth, 15s.

YOUNG WOMAN'S COMPANION. By Mrs. HEMANS. 10 Engravings on Steel. 8vo. cloth, 15s.

PRIZE MEDAL, INTERNATIONAL EXHIBITION, 1862, was awarded to Messrs. VIRTUE for the "publication of Weale's Series."

See *JURORS' REPORTS*,

CLASS XXIX.

CATALOGUE
OF
RUDIMENTARY, SCIENTIFIC, EDUCATIONAL, AND CLASSICAL WORKS,

FOR COLLEGES, HIGH AND ORDINARY SCHOOLS, AND SELF-INSTRUCTION;

ALSO FOR

MECHANICS' INSTITUTIONS, FREE LIBRARIES, &c. &c.,

PUBLISHED BY

VIRTUE BROTHERS & CO., 1, AMEN CORNER,
PATERNOSTER ROW.

* THE ENTIRE SERIES IS FREELY ILLUSTRATED ON WOOD AND STONE WHERE REQUISITE.

The Public are respectfully informed that the whole of the late Mr. WEALE'S *Publications, contained in the following Catalogue, have been purchased by* VIRTUE BROTHERS & CO., *and that all future Orders will be supplied by them at* 1, AMEN CORNER.

* Additional Volumes, by Popular Authors, are in Preparation.

RUDIMENTARY SERIES.

2. NATURAL PHILOSOPHY, by Charles Tomlinson. 1s.
12. PNEUMATICS, by Charles Tomlinson. 1s.
20. PERSPECTIVE, by George Pyne. 2s.
27. PAINTING; or, A GRAMMAR OF COLOURING, by G. Field. 2s.
40. GLASS STAINING, by Dr. M. A. Gessert, With an Appendix on the Art of Enamelling. 1s.

January, 1865.

SCIENTIFIC AND MECHANICAL WORKS.

41. PAINTING ON GLASS, from the German of Fromberg. 1s.
50. LAW OF CONTRACTS FOR WORKS AND SERVICES, by David Gibbons. 1s.
66. CLAY LANDS AND LOAMY SOILS, by J. Donaldson. 1s.
69. MUSIC, Treatise on, by C. C. Spencer. 2s.
71. THE PIANOFORTE INSTRUCTIONS, by C. C. Spencer. 1s.
72. RECENT FOSSIL SHELLS (A Manual of the Mollusca), by S. P. Woodward. 5s. 6d.
   In cloth boards, 6s. 6d.; half morocco, 7s. 6d.
79**. PHOTOGRAPHY, a Popular Treatise on, from the French of D. Van Monckhoven, by W. H. Thornthwaite. 1s. 6d.
96. ASTRONOMY, by the Rev. R. Main. 1s.
107. METROPOLITAN BUILDINGS ACT, and THE METROPOLITAN ACT FOR REGULATING THE SUPPLY OF GAS, with Notes, by D. Gibbons and R. Hesketh. 2s. 6d.
108. METROPOLITAN LOCAL MANAGEMENT ACTS. 1s. 6d.
108*. METROPOLIS LOCAL MANAGEMENT AMENDMENT ACT, 1862; with Notes and Index, 1s.
109. NUISANCES REMOVAL AND DISEASE PREVENTION ACT. 1s.
110. RECENT LEGISLATIVE ACTS applying to Contractors, Merchants, and Tradesmen. 1s.
113. USE OF FIELD ARTILLERY ON SERVICE, by Jaubert, translated by Lieut.-Col. H. H. Maxwell. 1s. 6d.
113*. MEMOIR ON SWORDS, by Marey, translated by Lieut.-Col. H. H. Maxwell. 1s.
140. OUTLINES OF MODERN FARMING, by R. Scott Burn. Vol. I.—Soils, Manures, and Crops. 2s.
141. ———————————————— Vol. II. Farming Economy, Historical and Practical. 3s.
142. ———————————————— Vol. III. Stock—Cattle, Sheep, and Horses. 2s. 6d.
145. ———————————————— Vol. IV. Management of the Dairy—Pigs—Poultry. 2s.
146. ———————————————— Vol. V. Utilisation of Town Sewage—Irrigation—Reclamation of Waste Land. 2s. 6d.
   The above 5 vols. bound in 2, cloth boards, 14s.
144. COMPOSITION AND PUNCTUATION, by J. Brenan. 1s.
151. A HANDY BOOK ON THE LAW OF FRIENDLY, INDUSTRIAL AND PROVIDENT, BUILDING AND LOAN SOCIETIES. With Copious Notes. By Nathaniel White, Esq. 1s.

VIRTUE BROTHERS & CO., 1, AMEN CORNER.

SCIENTIFIC AND MECHANICAL WORKS. 23

152. PRACTICAL HINTS FOR INVESTING MONEY: with an Explanation of the Mode of Transacting Business on the Stock Exchange. By Francis Playford, Sworn Broker. 1s.

PHYSICAL SCIENCE.

1. CHEMISTRY, by Prof. Fownes, including Agricultural Chemistry, for the use of Farmers. 1s.
3. GEOLOGY, by Major-Gen. Portlock. 1s. 6d.
4. MINERALOGY, with a Treatise on Mineral Rocks or Aggregates, by Dana. 2s.
7. ELECTRICITY, by Sir W. S. Harris. 1s. 6d.
7*. GALVANISM, ANIMAL AND VOLTAIC ELECTRICITY; by Sir W. S. Harris. 1s. 6d.
8. MAGNETISM, Exposition of, by Sir W. S. Harris. 3s. 6d.
11. ELECTRIC TELEGRAPH, History of, by E. Highton. 2s.
133. METALLURGY OF COPPER, by R. H. Lamborn. 2s.
134. METALLURGY OF SILVER AND LEAD, by R. H. Lamborn. 2s.
135. ELECTRO-METALLURGY, by A. Watt. 1s. 6d.
138. HANDBOOK OF THE TELEGRAPH, by R. Bond. 1s.
143. EXPERIMENTAL ESSAYS—On the Motion of Camphor and Modern Theory of Dew, by C. Tomlinson. 1s.

BUILDING AND ARCHITECTURE.

16. ARCHITECTURE, Orders of, by W. H. Leeds. 1s.
17. ——————— Styles of, by T. Bury. 1s. 6d.
18. ——————— Principles of Design, by E. L. Garbett. 2s.
22. BUILDING, the Art of, by E. Dobson. 1s.
23. BRICK AND TILE MAKING, by E. Dobson. 2s.
25. MASONRY AND STONE-CUTTING, by E. Dobson. 2s.
30. DRAINING AND SEWAGE OF TOWNS AND BUILDINGS, by G. D. Dempsey. 1s. 6d.
(With No. 29, DRAINAGE OF LAND, 2 vols. in 1, 2s. 6d.)

VIRTUE BROTHERS & CO., 1, AMEN CORNER.

35. BLASTING AND QUARRYING OF STONE, AND BLOW-ING UP OF BRIDGES, by Lt.-Gen. Sir J. Burgoyne. 1s. 6d.
36. DICTIONARY OF TERMS used by Architects, Builders, Engineers, Surveyors, &c. 4s.
  In cloth boards, 5s.; half morocco, 6s.
42. COTTAGE BUILDING, by C. B. Allen. 1s.
44. FOUNDATIONS and CONCRETE WORKS, by E. Dobson. 1s.
45. LIMES, CEMENTS. MORTARS, CONCRETE, MASTICS, &c., by G. R. Burnell. 1s.
57. WARMING AND VENTILATION, by C. Tomlinson. 3s.
83**. CONSTRUCTION OF DOOR LOCKS, by C. Tomlinson. 1s. 6d.
111. ARCHES, PIERS, AND BUTTRESSES, by W. Bland. 1s. 6d.
116. ACOUSTICS OF PUBLIC BUILDINGS, by T. R. Smith. 1s. 6d.
123. CARPENTRY AND JOINERY, founded on Robison and Tredgold. 1s. 6d.
123*. ILLUSTRATIVE PLATES to the preceding. 4to. 4s. 6d.
124. ROOFS FOR PUBLIC AND PRIVATE BUILDINGS, founded on Robison, Price, and Tredgold. 1s. 6d.
124*. IRON ROOFS of Recent Construction—Descriptive Plates. 4to. 4s. 6d.
127. ARCHITECTURAL MODELLING, Practical Instructions, by T. A. Richardson. 1s. 6d.
128. VITRUVIUS'S ARCHITECTURE, translated by J. Gwilt, with Plates. 5s.
130. GRECIAN ARCHITECTURE, Principles of Beauty in, by the Earl of Aberdeen. 1s.
132. ERECTION OF DWELLING-HOUSES, with Specifications, Quantities of Materials, &c., by S. H. Brooks, 27 Plates. 2s. 6d.

MACHINERY AND ENGINEERING.

33. CRANES AND MACHINERY FOR RAISING HEAVY BODIES, the Art of Constructing, by J. Glynn. 1s.
34. STEAM ENGINE, by Dr. Lardner. 1s.
43. TUBULAR AND IRON GIRDER BRIDGES, including the Britannia and Conway Bridges, by G. D. Dempsey. 1s.

VIRTUE BROTHERS & CO., 1, AMEN CORNER.

SCIENTIFIC AND MECHANICAL WORKS.

47. LIGHTHOUSES, their Construction and Illumination, by Allan Stevenson. 3s.
59. STEAM BOILERS, their Construction and Management, by R. Armstrong. 1s.
62. RAILWAYS, Construction, by Sir M. Stephenson. 1s. 6d.
62*. RAILWAY CAPITAL AND DIVIDENDS, with Statistics of Working, by E. D. Chattaway. 1s.
(Vols. 62 and 62* bound in 1, 2s. 6d.)
67. CLOCK AND WATCH MAKING, and Church Clocks and Bells, by E. B. Denison. 3s. 6d.
78. STEAM AND LOCOMOTION, on the Principle of connecting Science with Practice, by J. Sewell. 2s.
78*. LOCOMOTIVE ENGINES, by G. D. Dempsey. 1s. 6d.
79*. ILLUSTRATIONS TO THE ABOVE. 4to. 4s. 6d.
98. MECHANISM AND CONSTRUCTION OF MACHINES, by T. Baker; and TOOLS AND MACHINES, by J. Nasmyth, with 220 Woodcuts. 2s. 6d.
114. MACHINERY, Construction and Working, by C. D. Abel. 1s. 6d.
115. PLATES TO THE ABOVE. 4to. 7s. 6d.
139. STEAM ENGINE, Mathematical Theory of, by T. Baker. 1s.

CIVIL ENGINEERING, &c.

13. CIVIL ENGINEERING, by H. Law and G. R. Burnell. 4s. 6d.
29. DRAINING DISTRICTS AND LANDS, by G. D. Dempsey. 1s.
(With No. 30, DRAINAGE AND SEWAGE OF TOWNS, 2 vols. in 1, 2s. 6d.)
31. WELL-SINKING, BORING, AND PUMP WORK, by J. G. Swindell, revised by G. R. Burnell. 1s.
46. ROAD-MAKING AND MAINTENANCE OF MACADAMISED ROADS, by Gen. Sir J. Burgoyne. 1s. 6d.
60. LAND AND ENGINEERING SURVEYING, by T. Baker. 2s.

SCIENTIFIC AND MECHANICAL WORKS.

63. AGRICULTURAL ENGINEERING, BUILDINGS, MOTIVE POWERS, FIELD ENGINES, MACHINERY, AND IMPLEMENTS, by G. H. Andrews. 3s.

77*. ECONOMY OF FUEL, by T. S. Prideaux. 1s.

80*. EMBANKING LANDS FROM THE SEA, by J. Wiggins. 2s.

82. WATER POWER, as applied to Mills, &c., by J. Glynn. 2s.

82**. GAS WORKS AND MANUFACTURING COAL GAS, by S. Hughes. 3s.

82***. WATER-WORKS FOR CITIES AND TOWNS, by S. Hughes. 3s.

117. SUBTERRANEOUS SURVEYING, AND RANGING THE LINE without the Magnet, by T. Fenwick, with Additions by T. Baker. 2s. 6d.

118. CIVIL ENGINEERING OF NORTH AMERICA, by D. Stevenson. 3s.

120. HYDRAULIC ENGINEERING, by G. R. Burnell. 3s.

121. RIVERS AND TORRENTS, and a Treatise on NAVIGABLE CANALS AND RIVERS THAT CARRY SAND AND MUD, from the Italian of Paul Frisi. 2s. 6d.

125. COMBUSTION OF COAL, AND THE PREVENTION OF SMOKE, by C. Wye Williams, M.I.C.E. 3s.

SHIP-BUILDING AND NAVIGATION.

51. NAVAL ARCHITECTURE, by J. Peake. 3s.

53*. SHIPS FOR OCEAN AND RIVER SERVICE, Construction of, by Captain H. A. Sommerfeldt. 1s.

53**. ATLAS OF 15 PLATES TO THE ABOVE, Drawn for Practice. 4to. 7s. 6d.

54. MASTING, MAST-MAKING, and RIGGING OF SHIPS, by R. Kipping. 1s. 6d.

54*. IRON SHIP-BUILDING, by J. Grantham. 2s. 6d.

VIRTUE BROTHERS & CO., 1, AMEN CORNER.

54**. ATLAS OF 24 PLATES to the preceding. 4to. 22s. 6d.

55. NAVIGATION; the Sailor's Sea Book: How to Keep the Log and Work it off, &c.; Law of Storms, and Explanation of Terms, by J. Greenwood. 2s.

80. MARINE ENGINES, AND STEAM VESSELS, AND THE SCREW, by R. Murray. 2s. 6d.

83 bis. SHIPS AND BOATS, Forms of, by W. Bland. 1s.

99. NAUTICAL ASTRONOMY AND NAVIGATION, by J. R. Young. 2s.

100*. NAVIGATION TABLES, for Use with the above. 1s. 6d.

106. SHIPS' ANCHORS for all SERVICES, by G. Cotsell. 1s. 6d.

149. SAILS AND SAIL-MAKING, by R. Kipping, N.A. 2s. 6d.

ARITHMETIC AND MATHEMATICS.

6. MECHANICS, by Charles Tomlinson. 1s.

32. MATHEMATICAL INSTRUMENTS, THEIR CONSTRUCTION, USE, &c., by J. F. Heather. 1s.

61*. READY RECKONER for the Measurement of Land, Tables of Work at from 2s. 6d. to 20s. per acre, and valuation of Land from £1 to £1,000 per acre, by A. Arman. 1s. 6d.

76. GEOMETRY, DESCRIPTIVE, with a Theory of Shadows and Perspective, and a Description of the Principles and Practice of Isometrical Projection, by J. F. Heather. 2s.

83. BOOK-KEEPING AND COMMERCIAL PHRASEOLOGY, by James Haddon. 1s.

84. ARITHMETIC, with numerous Examples, by J.R. Young. 1s. 6d.

84*. KEY TO THE ABOVE, by J. R. Young. 1s. 6d.

VIRTUE BROTHERS & CO., 1, AMEN CORNER.

NEW SERIES OF EDUCATIONAL WORKS.

85. EQUATIONAL ARITHMETIC: Tables for the Calculation of Simple Interest, with Logarithms for Compound Interest, and Annuities, by W. Hipsley. 2s.
86. ALGEBRA, by J. Haddon. 2s.
86*. KEY AND COMPANION TO THE ABOVE, by J. R. Young. 1s. 6d.
88. EUCLID'S GEOMETRY, with Essay on Logic, by H. Law. 2s.
90. GEOMETRY, ANALYTICAL AND CONIC SECTIONS, by J. Hann. 1s.
91. PLANE TRIGONOMETRY, by J. Hann. 1s.
92. SPHERICAL TRIGONOMETRY, by J. Hann. 1s. (*The two volumes in one.* 2s.)
93. MENSURATION, by T. Baker. 1s.
94. LOGARITHMS, Tables of; with Tables of Natural Sines, Cosines, and Tangents, by H. Law. 2s. 6d.
97. STATICS AND DYNAMICS, by T. Baker. 1s.
101. DIFFERENTIAL CALCULUS, by W. S. B. Woolhouse. 1s.
101*. WEIGHTS AND MEASURES OF ALL NATIONS; Weights of Coins, and Divisions of Time; with the Principles which determine the Rate of Exchange, by W. S. B. Woolhouse. 1s. 6d.
102. INTEGRAL CALCULUS, by H. Cox. 1s.
103. INTEGRAL CALCULUS, Examples of, by J. Hann. 1s.
104. DIFFERENTIAL CALCULUS, Examples of, with Solutions, by J. Haddon. 1s.
105. ALGEBRA, GEOMETRY, and TRIGONOMETRY, First Mnemonical Lessons in, by the Rev. T. P. Kirkman. 1s. 6d.
131. READY-RECKONER FOR MILLERS, FARMERS, AND MERCHANTS, showing the Value of any Quantity of Corn, with the Approximate Value of Mill-stones and Mill Work. 1s.
136. RUDIMENTARY ARITHMETIC, by J. Haddon, edited by A. Arman. 1s. 6d.
137. KEY TO THE ABOVE, by A. Arman. 1s. 6d.
147. STEPPING STONE TO ARITHMETIC, by Abraham Arman, Schoolmaster, Thurleigh, Beds. 1s.
148. KEY TO THE ABOVE, by A. Arman. 1s.

VIRTUE BROTHERS & CO., 1, AMEN CORNER.

NEW SERIES OF EDUCATIONAL WORKS.

[*This Series is kept in three styles of binding—the prices of each are given in columns at the end of the lines.*]

HISTORIES, GRAMMARS, AND DICTIONARIES.	Limp.	Cloth Boards.	Half Morocco.
	s. d.	*s. d.*	*s. d.*
1. ENGLAND, History of, by W. D. Hamilton. Parts I., II. in 1 vol.	2 0		
3. ———— Parts III., IV. in 1 vol.	2 0		
———— Complete in 1 vol.	4 0	5 0	5 6
5. GREECE, History of, by W. D. Hamilton and E. Levien.	2 6	3 6	4 0
7. ROME, History of, by E. Levien.	2 6	3 6	4 0
9. CHRONOLOGY OF CIVIL AND ECCLEsiastical History, Literature, Art, and Civilisation, from the earliest period to the present time	2 6	3 6	4 0
11. ENGLISH GRAMMAR, by Hyde Clarke	1 0		
11*. HANDBOOK OF COMPARATIVE PHIlology, by Hyde Clarke	1 0		
12. ENGLISH DICTIONARY, above 100,000 words, or 50,000 more than in any existing work, by Hyde Clarke	3 6	4 6	5 0
————————————, with Grammar		5 6	6 0
14. GREEK GRAMMAR, by H. C. Hamilton	1 0		
15. ———— DICTIONARY, by H. R. Hamilton. Vol. 1. Greek—English	2 0		
17. ———— Vol. 2. English—Greek	2 0		
———— Complete in 1 vol.		5 0	5 6
————————————, with Grammar		6 0	6 6
19. LATIN GRAMMAR, by T. Goodwin	1 0		
20. ———— DICTIONARY, by T. Goodwin. Vol. 1. Latin—English	2 0		
22. ———— Vol. 2. English—Latin	1 6		
———— Complete in 1 vol.		4 6	5 0
————————————, with Grammar		5 6	6 0

VIRTUE BROTHERS & CO., 1, AMEN CORNER.

NEW SERIES OF EDUCATIONAL WORKS.

HISTORIES, GRAMMARS, AND DICTIONARIES.	Limp.	Cloth Boards.	Half Morocco.
	s. d.	s. d.	s. d.
24. FRENCH GRAMMAR, by G. L. Strauss	1 0		
25. ———— DICTIONARY, by A. Elwes. Vol. 1. French—English	1 0		
26. ———————— Vol. 2. English—French	1 6		
———— Complete in 1 vol.		3 6	4 0
————————, with Grammar		4 6	5 0
27. ITALIAN GRAMMAR, by A. Elwes	1 0		
28. ———— TRIGLOT DICTIONARY, by A. Elwes. Vol. 1. Italian — English — French	2 0		
30. ———— Vol. 2. English—Italian—French	2 0		
32. ———— Vol. 3. French—Italian—English	2 0		
———— Complete in 1 vol.		7 6	8 6
————————, with Grammar		8 6	9 6
34. SPANISH GRAMMAR, by A. Elwes	1 0		
35. ———— ENGLISH AND ENGLISH-SPANISH DICTIONARY, by A. Elwes	4 0	5 0	5 6
————————, with Grammar		6 0	6 6
39. GERMAN GRAMMAR, by G. L. Strauss	1 0		
40. ———— READER, from best Authors	1 0		
41. ———— TRIGLOT DICTIONARY, by N. E. Hamilton. Vol. 1. English—German—French	1 0		
42. ———— Vol. 2. German—English—French	1 0		
43. ———— Vol. 3. French—English—German	1 0		
———— Complete in 1 vol.	3 0	4 0	4 6
————————, with Grammar		5 0	5 6
44. HEBREW DICTIONARY, by Dr. Breslau. Vol. 1. Hebrew—English	7 0		
46. ———— Vol. 2. English—Hebrew	3 0		
———— Complete, with Grammar, in 2 vols.		12 0	14 0
46*. ———— GRAMMAR, by Dr. Breslau	1 0		
47. FRENCH AND ENGLISH PHRASE BOOK	1 0		

VIRTUE BROTHERS & CO., 1, AMEN CORNER.

GREEK AND LATIN CLASSICS,

With Explanatory Notes in English, principally selected from the best German Commentators.

LATIN SERIES.

1. LATIN DELECTUS, with Vocabularies and Notes, by H. Young . . . . 1s.
2. CÆSAR'S GALLIC WAR; Notes by H. Young . . 2s.
3. CORNELIUS NEPOS; Notes by H. Young . . . 1s.
4. VIRGIL. The Georgics, Bucolics; Notes by W. Rushton and H. Young . . . . 1s.
5. VIRGIL'S ÆNEID; Notes by H. Young . . . 2s.
6. HORACE. Odes and Epodes; Notes, Analysis and Explanation of Metres . . . . 1s.
7. HORACE. Satires and Epistles; Notes by W. B. Smith 1s. 6d.
8. SALLUST. Catiline, Jugurtha; Notes by W. M. Donne 1s. 6d.
9. TERENCE. Andria and Heautontimorumenos; Notes by J. Davies . . . . 1s. 6d.
10. TERENCE. Adelphi, Hecyra, and Phormio; Notes by J. Davies . . . . 2s.
14. CICERO. De Amicitia, de Senectute, and Brutus; Notes by W. B. Smith . . . . 2s.
16. LIVY. Part I. Books i., ii., by H. Young . . 1s. 6d.
16*. ——— Part II. Books iii., iv., v., by H. Young . 1s. 6d.
17. ——— Part III. Books xxi., xxii., by W. B. Smith . 1s.
19. CATULLUS, TIBULLUS, OVID, and PROPERTIUS, Selections from, by W. M. Donne . . . . 2s.
20. SUETONIUS and the later Latin Writers, Selections from, by W. M. Donne . . . . 2s.

Preparing for Press.

11. CICERO. Orations against Catiline, for Sulla, for Archias, and for the Manilian Law.
12. CICERO. First and Second Philippics; Orations for Milo, for Marcellus, &c.
13. CICERO. De Officiis.
15. JUVENAL and PERSIUS. (The indelicate passages expunged.)
18. TACITUS. Agricola; Germania; and Annals, Book i.

VIRTUE BROTHERS & CO., 1, AMEN CORNER.

GREEK SERIES,

ON A SIMILAR PLAN TO THE LATIN SERIES.

1. GREEK INTRODUCTORY READER, by H. Young.
On the same plan as the Latin Reader . . . . 1s.
2. XENOPHON. Anabasis, i. ii. iii., by H. Young . . 1s.
3. XENOPHON. Anabasis, iv. v. vi. vii., by H. Young . 1s.
4. LUCIAN. Select Dialogues, by T. H. L. Leary . . 1s.
5. HOMER. Iliad, i. to vi., by T. H. L. Leary . . 1s. 6d.
6. HOMER. Iliad, vii. to xii., by T. H. L. Leary . 1s. 6d.
7. HOMER. Iliad, xiii. to xviii., by T. H. L. Leary . 1s. 6d.
8. HOMER. Iliad, xix. to xxiv., by T. H. L. Leary . 1s. 6d.
9. HOMER. Odyssey, i. to vi., by T. H. L. Leary . 1s. 6d.
10. HOMER. Odyssey, vii. to xii., by T. H. L. Leary . 1s. 6d.
11. HOMER. Odyssey, xiii. to xviii., by T. H. L. Leary 1s. 6d.
12. HOMER. Odyssey, xix. to xxiv.; and Hymns, by T. H. L. Leary . . . . 2s.
13. PLATO. Apology, Crito, and Phædo, by J. Davies . . 2s.
14. HERODOTUS, i. ii., by T. H. L. Leary . . . 1s. 6d.
15. HERODOTUS, iii. iv., by T. H. L. Leary . . . 1s. 6d.
16. HERODOTUS, v. vi. vii., by T. H. L. Leary . . 1s. 6d.
17. HERODOTUS, viii. ix., and Index, by T. H. L. Leary 1s. 6d.
18. SOPHOCLES; Œdipus Tyrannus, by H. Young . . 1s.
20. SOPHOCLES; Antigone, by J. Milner . . . . 2s.
23. EURIPIDES; Hecuba and Medea, by W. B. Smith . 1s. 6d.
26. EURIPIDES; Alcestis, by J. Milner . . . . 1s.
30. ÆSCHYLUS; Prometheus Vinctus, by J. Davies . . 1s.
32. ÆSCHYLUS; Septem contra Thebas, by J. Davies . . 1s.
40. ARISTOPHANES; Acharnians, by C. S. D. Townsend 1s. 6d.
41. THUCYDIDES, i., by H. Young . . . . . 1s.

" *Preparing for Press.*

19. SOPHOCLES; Œdipus Colonæus.
21. SOPHOCLES; Ajax.
22. SOPHOCLES; Philoctetes.
25. EURIPIDES; Hippolytus.
27. EURIPIDES; Orestes.
28. EURIPIDES. Extracts from the remaining plays.
29. SOPHOCLES. Extracts from the remaining plays.
31. ÆSCHYLUS: Persæ.
33. ÆSCHYLUS; Choëphoræ.
34. ÆSCHYLUS; Eumenides.
35. ÆSCHYLUS; Agamemnon.
36. ÆSCHYLUS; Supplices.
37. PLUTARCH; Select Lives.
38. ARISTOPHANES; Clouds.
39. ARISTOPHANES; Frogs.
42. THUCYDIDES, ii.
43. THEOCRITUS; Select Idyls.
44. PINDAR.
45. ISOCRATES.
46. HESIOD.

VIRTUE BROTHERS & CO., 1, AMEN CORNER.

www.ingramcontent.com/pod-product-compliance
Lightning Source LLC
Chambersburg PA
CBHW020908230426
43666CB00008B/1368